CONTENTS

PRO TACTICS™

WALLEYE

PRO TACTICS™

WALLEYE

Use the Secrets of the Pros to
Catch More and Bigger Walleye

Mark Martin

THE LYONS PRESS
Guilford, Connecticut
An imprint of The Globe Pequot Press

To my dad, who never tired of taking me fishing!
Thank you.

The Lyons Press is an imprint of The Globe Pequot Press.
Pro Tactics is a trademark of Morris Book Publishing, LLC.

Text design by Peter Holm, Sterling Hill Productions

Library of Congress Cataloging-in-Publication Data is available.

ISBN 978-1-59921-256-2

Printed in the United States of America

10 9 8 7 6 5 4 3 2 1

ACKNOWLEDGMENTS

I want to thank the following people who helped make this book possible: Dave Scroppo, Dave Rose, Mike Gofron, Mark Brumbaugh, Ross Grothe, Dave Anderson, Sam Anderson, Gary Roach, and Al Lindner. And thanks to everyone else with whom I have had the pleasure of sharing the art of fishing—the knowledge flows both ways.

Four Seasons of Walleye

As I look back on last year, to say nothing of a couple decades of walleye fishing, it's easy to see the trends that emerge from one season to another. Spring through winter, walleyes make predictable movements, heading to the shallows for a few months before sliding back to the depths. The better you follow them, the better your chances for success. That's why we're going to look at the four seasons and the prevailing patterns for each of them. Consider this your most important calendar—a "cheat sheet" to lead you through the months and to more walleyes.

Spring: Storm the Shallows

Spring walleyes invade the shallows to spawn and then hang around for a spell before dispersing. Few other movements are as predictable as this one, and I like to narrow my search by looking for current. If there's a river, there will be walleyes around. Up on Lake of the Woods, fish sift into the Rainy River. Off of Erie, they slide up the Detroit. On any number of smaller waters, they stage off creeks and narrows—any place with current. Additional keys to locating spring walleyes are weeds, drop-offs, and gravelly, hard-bottom areas. In rivers, concentrations of walleyes will hold below dams and current breaks, including pilings, rock piles, and dips and valleys in the bottom.

Jigging always excels in spring. You can pitch jigs shallow or fish them vertically below the boat. Bring minnows, leeches, and crawlers—it's never too early for leeches and crawlers. Many times I'll hook two smaller minnows on a jig, with one right side up and the other upside down. Together they look like a V for a greater profile with more flash. And when there's competition from numbers of fish, if a walleye steals one of the minnows, you still have another one ready to catch its buddy.

Other options are casting minnow baits such as Countdown Rapalas or trolling Original Rapalas over the shallows. In rivers, trolling is too often overlooked. To find fish I'll pull Storm Hot 'n' Tots upstream and down. But when you go downstream, be sure to shorten the length of your line. After you find the fish, you can often go back and mop up on them with jigs.

This walleye was caught while pitching jigs in shallow water around rocks and weeds. DAVID ROSE

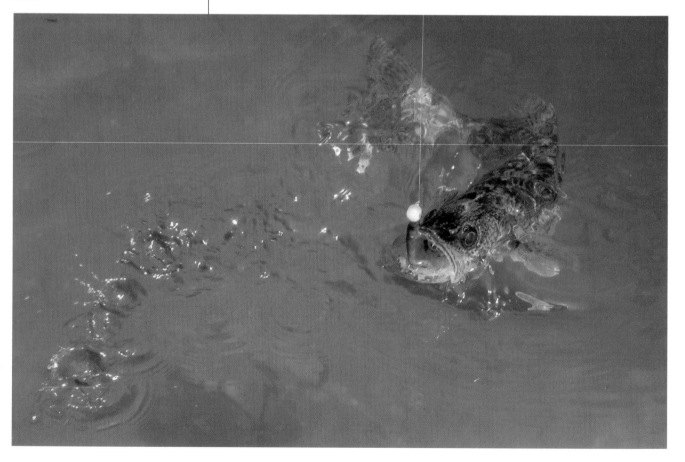

Summer: Break Out the Lead

When summertime sets in, there's no more efficient way to find fish—and catch them—than with bottom bouncers and spinners. They not only cover water but also combine the strum of an artificial with the smell and taste of live bait.

As in ice fishing, I don't limit myself to just prominent structures. I'll look well beyond them in the lake basin or in a reservoir's deepest creek channels. Since you can bet most of the fish will be in more than 20 feet of water, the best way to find them is with quality electronics. In fact, I seldom start fishing without seeing anything on my electronics. That way you'll see bugs, bait, and predators. Don't be afraid to spend time just looking.

While bottom bouncers keep bait near bottom, they also tell you a lot about it. When I use a bottom bouncer on Berkley FireLine (most often twenty-pound), I can feel the sponge of soft bottom and the "tick-tick" of hard bottom. Focus on these changes, since food such as crayfish, minnows, and aquatic insects will concentrate there. Still, the fish will change location from day to day, even hour to hour. You have to keep moving along the structure and beyond it to stay on fish. If, on the other hand, I spot walleyes up higher on my electronics, I'll set back a spinner with a nightcrawler behind a planer board. To get it down to the appropriate depth, I'll use either a bouncer or a clip-on weight.

It's also important to experiment with your spinners. While the guidelines of silver in clear water and gold in dark hold true, you'll often find certain preferences depending on the water. Come midsummer, walleyes feed a surprising amount on crayfish, and the best pattern I've found to trigger fish is gold with a splash of orange—even in clear water. No. 2 and No. 3 blades do the job most places, but if you get around big fish or on the Great Lakes, boost up

Spinner and nightcrawler strike again. DAVID SCROPPO

to No. 4 and No. 5. Stock up on a variety of blades and try different sizes and colors, including the new generation of holographic offerings, which often outproduce hammered or standard blades. The more you test, the better your grade will be.

Fall: Head for the Narrows

Want to zero in on walleyes when the water cools? Then head for the narrows. The quickest shortcut to find fall fish is to work areas between lakes or with any kind of current. Channels leading from one lake to another, inlets, and rivers or the mouths of bays are all prime territory.

When I get there, I look for green weeds that hold baitfish. In shallow water no deeper than 12 feet, walleyes often will be concentrated due to the food and a slight stain in clarity that comes with current. Current, though, doesn't necessarily mean a river—wind can create it, too. Fish on the downwind sides of points, where bait washes in, and be ready.

To target walleyes when the water dips into the 50s or below, I know of no better way than with crankbaits. Large Rapala Husky Jerks—nothing smaller than No. 10 and preferably a No. 14—trip a predator's trigger when it's feeding on the season's biggest baitfish. Fishing jerkbaits on FireLine for its lack of stretch, I cast out, reel the bait down, and stop it. Sometimes you can let it sit until you get a hit. If you don't, work it in with twitches of the rod tip and frequent pauses. When you catch a fish, make a mental note of the length of the pause and repeat it. When the fish stop biting one particular retrieve, begin experimenting. Another great bait in fall is the Rapala Tail Dancer, which you can cast out and reel in slowly, punctuating the retrieve with occasional twitches.

Winter: Expand Your Reach

If anything, it's too easy to return to the same old, same old when ice fishing—you know, park your coop in one place and don't budge for months. Make a resolution, then, to expand on your locations and techniques for winter walleyes.

For starters, gear up with the best in modern-day technology. With it, you won't stay put on the ice. A high-quality auger punches holes in no time, allowing you to drop a line here, there, and everywhere in order to cover more hard water. Beyond the auger, consider investing in an underwater camera. You'll be able to watch fish move in—heck, you'll be able to verify their presence in the first place—and adjust jigging motions to trigger them. Usually walleyes race in but then require a lighter jigging motion to make them bite. With a camera, you'll be able to see if you twitch a jig or a spoon too hard—the walleyes will skate away in a flash.

This is also the time of year to go deep, my dear. When you set up near a reef or an underwater point or bar, be sure to explore the areas out from it where the bottom changes from hard to soft and tapers into the lake basin. It's worth your while to have a number of holes drilled so you can stair-step your way out to the deepest water in the lake.

But not all fish are on bottom. Even over 30 feet of water, I like to set a tip-up at varying depths, changing its level about every half hour. I might start with a bait halfway down, then extend it to 20 feet a little later. You'll be surprised how many walleyes suspend in winter.

If you're working two holes in front of you, work one with a Jigging Rapala or a spoon. For the other, set up a dead rod with a jig and minnow. Just let it sit there, and watch the rod tip bounce as the minnow quivers. When it stops, reach over and bump the rod to get the minnow dancing again. Often your jigging action will bring the fish in, but they'll take the bait on the dead rod. When you diversify in wintertime, the walleyes will reward you.

When you follow the prevailing patterns throughout the year, you'll stay on fish no matter the season. So put this story in your memory bank or even in your pocket. It will help you put the principles into practice spring, summer, fall, or winter.

Here, I'm moving slowly along structure trying to locate fish with my electronics. DAVID ROSE

SPRING

CHAPTER ONE

Rigged and Ready

A tricked-out boat delivers in spades.

Rigging a boat is one thing. Tricking it out is another. And in the interest of function, performance, and safety, a tricked-out boat delivers in spades. So does caring for it with a measure of preventive maintenance.

Whether a boat is a new one or an old friend, it deserves some attention before you go down the road and out on the water. And either one would benefit as well—you would, too—from some of the newest, slickest options for rigging or retrofitting. Your boat will thank you.

Lubrication

To get started, well before I hit the road, I give the trailer and boat a look-see. Toolbox in tow, I check nuts, bolts, and screws everywhere—even on the boat itself—tightening anything that needs it.

Next up, take care of everything on the lubrication front. For this I depend on synthetic lubricant for all parts of boat and trailer. Look for a spray you can spritz on any electrical connection to provide a rust inhibitor. Hit the connections to batteries, trailer lights, electronics, and trolling motor. Speaking of batteries, life is even easier in that department with the new maintenance-free models. Checking water levels, however seldom you needed to with traditional batteries, is now a thing of the past.

For a heavier dose of lube where it's deserved—say, on trailer hubs or zerks (the nubs that supply lubrication to the steering apparatus of your boat's motor)—try a synthetic lubricant derived from PTFE, a key ingredient in Teflon. It does its job in a grease gun, replacing old-fashioned petroleum-based grease.

Stem to Stern

In the interest of safety, I have my kicker motor rigged with a power lift, which tilts or deploys the motor at a touch of a button. That's a handy option to have when the waves are rolling and it would be difficult to perch back near the transom to lift that trolling motor by hand.

While you're stocking or supplying your boat with all the necessary items, don't forget a good anchor and at least 100 feet of anchor rope in case your motor goes on the fritz. Another handy thing to have aboard is a drift sock. Tie it to 20 to 30 feet of rope, and it's great for slowing your boat while fishing in wind. It's also indispensable in times of peril—say, if your motor goes down in high winds and waves. The reason is that you can tie the sock to the bow eyelet on that length of rope, and it will keep the boat's bow into the wind rather than having it turn sideways to the swells, where it could swamp.

In case the water gets hairy, a couple more items to have on board are safety flares (if you've had yours for a while, check to see how old they are) and a signaling flag. The bright-orange flag should be aboard—in fact it's law on some waters, including the Ohio portion of Lake Erie—to provide another signal for help.

An ounce of prevention can help protect your equipment and yourself for the long term. Anytime, for that matter, is a good time to give your boat and trailer a once-over. Hit electrical connections, and then stow a drift sock for fishing and in the event your boat goes floating for the middle of nowhere in high seas. It would be a shame to miss a great catch because your boat wasn't both rigged and ready.

CHAPTER TWO

Spring Has Sprung

Recent weather will impact your plans.

Come March and April, you had better figure the recent weather into your plans. If it's a cold spring, the walleyes probably won't start spawning in mid-March and do their dispersal with the early-spring advance of warm weather. Instead they'll likely start spawning in April and will hang tight to the same areas for the next few weeks. That holds true wherever you are, although the farther north you live or fish, the later the spawn and the opener. If it's an early spring, on the other hand, it pays to look farther down the river or lake, on points and flats near but not next to spawning grounds.

Where to look? Walleyes are opportunists that will spawn in rock, gravel, and weeds. In the same body of water, you might find walleyes over some of each. Check all of them, as well as the adjacent areas—walleyes that have spawned in 3 to 5 feet of water over weeds might be just offshore where the water gets deeper. Or they might be on a nearby patch of sand and gravel. Or they could be just a cast away from a small creek. The clearer the water, the deeper you'll have to look. Some days you have to look beyond the drop-off on mud bottoms that warm first in clear water and generate the earliest insect life.

If the weeks of weather *before* you hit the water are important, so are the conditions on the day you're out there. Often it's no problem to catch fish all night long, but when darkness gives way to light, it can be difficult to trigger any of the fish during the first few hours of daylight as their systems adjust. Sunlight and warmer midday temperatures can be the key to fish activity. By the time noon rolls around and the sun has been on the water a few hours, walleyes will often begin moving shallow and feeding. On dark, windy days without the warming effect, the fish will often hold deeper and be less active.

The Tag Team

Whenever I've found potential spawning areas, I start the search with a pair of lures. I know of no more effective way of covering water than with a tag-team approach—one angler pitching a crankbait and another using a jig.

The best cranks in spring are on the small side, something 4 inches or less. It's hard to beat an Original No. 9 or No. 11 Rapala cast and retrieved over gravel, rocks, and weeds. This time of year, walleyes are more reluctant to smash a mouthful, like a big jerkbait, and are more prone to pop something more delicate. To fish a floating Rap, cast out, crank it a few times to get it down and skim the weeds, then work it in with a slow retrieve punctuated by pauses and twitches. A 7-foot spinning rod is an excellent choice for throwing lures long distances and setting hooks.

Meanwhile, the other angler complements the crank with a slower offering to get the less-aggressive fish. Enter $\frac{1}{16}$- and $\frac{1}{8}$-ounce jigheads, great choices for working live bait. If you're in water 10 feet or less, you're going to want to pitch it out and work it back slowly to the boat. Be sure to mix up your retrieves and find what does the trick—and that key little motion might change day to day, even hour to hour. Many days nothing is more effective than a simple drag, where you pull the jig and bait along bottom. But when the water warms during midday, you can get a little more aggressive and lift and drop the jig, pop it, maybe shake it in place. Make a mental note, though, of what you're doing when you get bit. Now's

Opposite: Slowly lifting and dropping a Fireball jig enticed this walleye. DAVID ROSE

the time to replicate that action. Fish will often be into the same retrieve. When they stop biting, however, I'll switch colors or bait. Or sometimes I'll slip deeper and fish vertically.

Often, vertical fishing is about all you can do on rivers where the bottom is strewn with snags. Always try to keep your jig straight up and down below the boat. If necessary, boost up to a bigger jig than you might normally use. It's more important to be vertical than to try to finesse bites with a lighter jig that might slip off on an angle below the boat. Pay attention, too, to how much you lift and drop a jig. I always try to stay within 6 inches of bottom. That's where the fish will be, lying behind obstructions out of the current.

For fishing straight below the boat or dragging upstream, you need the right equipment to get the most out of your jig. The rod, trolling motor, and even the boat work together in a single package for most effective presentation. Here I suggest you downsize to the 6-foot, 2-inch model for better control. Meanwhile, a powerful electric motor is key for cranking up the amps and hovering over the fish in wind. In wind you might need to go with a quarter-ounce jig to stay vertical in 15 feet or less.

When it comes to scoring big fish in the washout holes below dams or behind pilings—spring walleyes hold behind any obstruction that breaks current—one of my killer presentations is a sizable jig with a sizable minnow. This offering often works best for the big hens and fends off some of the smaller males. In current I like to take a ⅜- or ⅝-ounce Northland Whistler jig, which is flat-sided to cut current, and break the propeller off. The narrow, hydrodynamic jighead cuts current and allows for better contact with bottom. If snags are few, I'll hold the jig just an inch or two off bottom when slipping current. If current is slow, I'll sometimes move slowly upstream with a bowmount trolling motor and drag the jig. There's something about the lack of action on a big jig that triggers the females.

In spring this lack of speed is often critical. You seldom need to hop the jig aggressively. Usually a 2- to 5-inch lift and drop is plenty. Bait, on the other hand, can play an important role. Minnows are a great starting point, since walleyes recuperating from the spawn, particularly the bigger ones, turn first to the essential amino acids found in minnows and leeches. As a backup plan, I bring leeches, but they can be troublesome in the cold water. To acclimate them to the temperature of the lake or river water, I put my leeches in a mesh bag, which I put in the live well. The bag not

only scrapes the critters of their crud and breathes life into them but also lets them adjust to the water temperature in my live or bait well. This way they won't ball up when they hit the cold spring water.

Try to focus your efforts in places adjacent to spawning areas, with a mind to the recent weather. If you do, and approach the walleyes with a tag-team effort, you're going to find more of them. Sure, everything could change again by next year, but if you follow the strategy outlined above, you're going to have far better success than if you relied on your newly minted memories.

Opposite: Working the deeper water adjacent to the walleyes' spawning area yields good results. DAVID ROSE

CHAPTER THREE

Gimme a Break(line)

Breaklines help to focus fish— and fishing efforts.

Look at the water and what do you see? At a glance there's water, water, everywhere. But upon closer inspection you'll see far more—the twists and turns in the drop-off that are visible with polarized glasses and deeper edges that are decipherable with electronics.

In short, the breaklines—the drop-offs that are like stair steps or ledges, from shallow to deep—are the place to be when walleye season opens. Attention to their detail is much more important, and effective, than floating around willy-nilly, following other boats or trying where you caught some fish last summer. It's spring, and the walleyes are close to their spawning grounds on the all-important breaks. You should be there, too.

Shallow First, Then Deep

So often in walleye fishing, folks think about superdeep water—places in the middle of the lake. That's all good and well—in summer. But in March and April walleyes are going to be much closer to shallow water. In fact, you'll get an idea of potential fishing spots simply by looking at the water, although polarized glasses are a huge help in getting a better picture of a spot's potential. Putting on a pair of polarized sunglasses, I'm able to cut the glare off the water and get a better look at the first breakline. When the water is clear, you'll be able to not only see that drop-off but also to spot little points and turns that hold fish. Walleyes concentrate at breaklines, especially when they are close to spawning grounds around creeks or points and flats with gravel bottom.

That's just one of the levels to check. The next is out just a bit deeper, where you'll typically find a secondary break that then gives way to even deeper water. I like to look for that next break with color electronics that show the change in depth and also have a brighter display of reds and yellows indicating harder bottom. When I find a little patch of hard bottom, I'll hover over it in my boat, since that's where walleyes tend to hold. It could be a patch of freshwater clams, even hard-packed sand. Difference is good.

Minnows, Rigs, Jigs

On the shallower breaks, you have choices in the ways to fish them. Nothing could be simpler than the first way: using a simple hook with a split-shot above it. Even if the water is quite shallow—say, 5 to 7 feet—you can long-line drift for walleyes. Take a No. 4 or No. 2 red hook, bait up with a minnow, and pinch on a split-shot a couple of feet above it. Pitch it out and then drift, watching for clumps of weeds or little holes—anything different that could hold fish. Watch the water temperature, too—an increase of even a couple of degrees will hold more fish, and more active ones. I like to run that split-shot rig on an ultralight rod and a reel spooled with soft monofilament. Four- or six-pound test is more than enough.

Another option for the shallow fish is to cast a jig on them when you see dark spots on the flat. (Often the dark spots are weeds or bottom that will hold a pocket of slightly warmer water.) Again, it's hard to beat a minnow. Rig it up on a 1/16-ounce jig, which is nice and light and drops so slowly that walleyes often eat it on the way down.

If the shallow fish aren't hitting—you'll find out in a drift or two—I move out to the next level, where I'll run the tried-and-true slip-sinker rig. (In clear water I often go with invisible fluorocarbon for my leader.) Out here I like to run my bowmount electric motor to hang on the break at a specific level and to hold steady in wind.

CHAPTER FOUR

Casting Cranks

Rod in hand, fish on the line.

When walleyes scatter throughout lakes with spring's progression—deep, suspended, and shallow—one segment of the population is hopped up, happy, and ready to lash out at aggressively worked lures. Why wait around with a bobber or bait rig when you can get fish with something far more active that better matches their late-spring mood?

Yes, I'm more inclined to seek walleyes out instead of letting them come to me. June is prime time for such an approach, since the water has warmed and the fish's activity level has increased. In other words, it's perfect for casting crankbaits to emerging weed beds, around points, and over flats. When the walleyes turn more aggressive, so can you.

Shallow Searching

Casting crankbaits is effective and enjoyable for a couple of reasons. For one, it covers water. A single cast reaches out, say, 100 feet, compared with

a bobber or live-bait rig that pretty much stays put. Meanwhile, it's a lot of fun to have a walleye whack a lure on superline—for both the intensity of the strike and the excitement of the fight.

When I look for shallow walleyes in late spring, I like relatively flat areas with 6 to 12 feet of water not too far from a deeper basin. To search for such water, you can idle with an outboard or from the front platform of your boat. To do the latter at relatively high speed, put down the bowmount trolling motor for steering purposes and put the outboard in gear. This provides extra elevation that, when complemented with polarized sunglasses, gives you a better vantage point for looking in the water and spotting weeds, rocks, even fish.

Whether you're up on the bow or at your console watching electronics, you're going to see subtle changes that hold fish. Could be a patch of weeds, boulders, or logs. In any case, I like to punch in GPS icons on the slight differences that hold fish. If I catch one or more walleye, I punch in an icon to mark fish or fish holding so that I can return later. Even the slightest underwater changes can hold walleyes.

Lures and Line

Now that you know what to look for, it's time to find the fish. I do it with my favorite search bait, a Rapala Shad Rap. The original balsa shads cast well on spinning tackle, and the plastic models that suspend—the RS (rattling and suspending) versions—are a touch heavier for bombing out long distances. The jointed models have enough weight for casting and the serious action walleyes love. No matter the bottom, if I bump it I'm going to rip back on my crank—not only to free it but also to provide the burst of speed that walleyes love.

It's almost impossible to do that without FireLine. Berkley FireLine has zero stretch and plentiful strength in eight- or ten-pound versions suited to casting with spinning tackle. I pair the reel with a 6-foot, 6-inch or 7-foot medium-action rod that has enough flex to let a walleye inhale a crank but enough backbone to help bounce a lure out of weeds and rocks.

Opposite: Casting cranks along this steep ledge allowed me to cover water faster and to find active fish faster. DAVID ROSE

Subtlety Makes Sense

A few more subtleties pay big dividends when casting cranks. One is to vary retrieve speed. Sure, you'll catch fish chucking and winding, but you're going to catch more if you add a few twitches of the rod tip or give the reel two rotations, stop, and then add a few more cranks.

You'll also find the nuances that attract walleyes using the electronic mapping chips from Navionics. They'll help you see rocks and hard bottom denoted on the map that pops up on your GPS unit. You'll also see points connected to flats and tighter contour lines that indicate sharper drop-offs. All are worth extra attention.

The bottom line is that casting crankbaits is a fun, aggressive way to fish walleyes. Bait is great, but casting cranks can be better.

CHAPTER FIVE

Drift Sock Strategies

How to use "water parachutes" to slow a boat in wind.

What are you going to do when the wind rips and the water gets wild? Are you going to surrender and head back to the dock?

If safety's a concern, returning to shore is the right decision. If discomfort and sloppy, frustrating fishing presentations have more to do with your decision, there's a solution—drift bags, otherwise known as drift socks or wind socks. Whatever you call them, they are indispensable pieces of equipment to control a boat in high winds and to provide pinpoint precision in more moderate conditions.

With new designs and materials, modern-generation drift bags do a much better job of controlling a boat. You can count on their durability, their range of sizes for different situations, and their applicability to drifting and trolling. They not only slow a boat in a tempest but also steady the craft and keep it in the fish zone.

The Parachute Effect

From a construction standpoint, modern socks have several things going for them. For one, they are made from a durable nylon that is impervious to rot. They also deploy in a flash, meaning they open and start slowing the boat without your having to monkey with them. Look for a model with a separate drawstring for dumping water out of it—making it a breeze (pardon the pun) to pull in without hauling on hundreds of pounds of water.

Since the bags are available in a variety of diameters—20, 30, 40, 50, and 60 inches—I always have the right tool for the job. For controlled drifting, I pick a model depending on the conditions. For example, for a 20-foot walleye boat I use a 50-inch bag when it's extremely rough, the 40-incher when conditions are a bit more moderate, and the 20-incher to make minor adjustments. Most of the time I point my trolling motor away

Drift bags allow for more controlled drifting or trolling.
DAVID ROSE

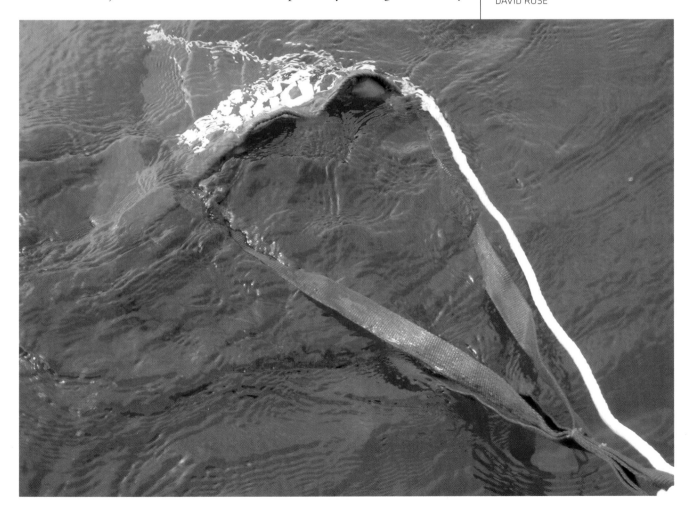

from the break or bottom I want to fish, because the wind is going to blow me into it. Then I put out the bag on the upwind bow cleat. The weight of the motor in the back of the boat is usually sufficient to keep the tail of the boat from swinging in the wind. Still, at times I've attached the 50-incher to the front cleat, the 40-incher to the middle, and the 20-incher closer to the stern.

Believe it or not, I've been able to slow the boat from 5 mph to less than 1 mph with the socks. This makes it possible to fish a ⅛-ounce jig or a ¼-ounce bottom bouncer even in 35- to 45-mile-per-hour winds—just the kinds of punishing conditions possible, even probable, in the tournaments I fish. What's also great about drift bags is that they keep the boat from rocking in the wind; they provide stability and keep the bowmount trolling motor's prop in the water. Team a powerful trolling motor with more than a hundred pounds of thrust with quality deep-cycle batteries, and you'll be able to fish all day whatever the conditions.

Although there is some debate regarding how close to keep the bags to the boat when drifting, I try to keep them as close as possible so that they open up and keep the boat from rocking. The short leash and less play in the rope make it easier to reel a fish around the bags and keep from tangling.

Slow for a Troll

Drift socks are an angling solution not only for drifting but also for trolling. With a bag connected to the bow eyelet, let the bag run underneath the boat. Just make sure the line isn't too long and that it doesn't allow the bag to get into the motor. (On a 20-foot boat, I use about a 15-foot line.)

I've seen situations on Lake Erie, Saginaw Bay, and reservoirs of the Dakotas when wind pushes a boat at trolling speeds that are far too fast. Another problem is the surge that enters the picture when a boat reaches a wave crest and surfs down, yanking lines ahead with herky-jerky motion that diminishes a smooth presentation and rips hooks from fish. With bags tied to the front cleats to keep the bow in the water and bags just ahead of the transom, you'll slow your speed without tangling the bag in the motor. You'll probably slow the speed too much, which is perfect. You can now run your kicker motor and actually steer despite the rough conditions.

When you're able to turn up the RPMs on your kicker motor, you'll have sufficient torque to turn and follow your intended path. And instead of surging from 0.9 to 1.7 mph, you're now able to keep your progress nice and smooth.

With this bag setup I'm also able to troll back upwind if the waves are less than 3 feet—again, because the bow stays in and slices the water. If I've trolled downwind and want to return through a pod of fish, I make a wide, slow turn and then start up my main outboard. With the bags, my big motor will troll at speeds as low as 1 mph.

I say don't wave the white flag when you don't have to. With drift socks you can keep fishing efficiently in difficult conditions—just the ticket to save the tournament day or vital time on your annual walleye vacation. You couldn't do it without them.

CHAPTER SIX

The Road to Nowhere

Principles of open water.

Learn the principles of open water on a huge lake like Erie, and you'll be ready to take the technique anywhere in walleye country.

When you're walleye fishing, sometimes there's no place like the middle of nowhere. We're talking far from any underwater point, hump, or weed bed. We're talking far from flats, creek channels, or any bottom-altering oddity that has fish written all over it on electronics. Yes, we're talking walleyes in the middle of nowhere, open-water roamers that chase bait partly down in the water column across miles of vast expanses.

Daunting? Maybe at first. Incredibly productive? You bet.

The best open-water walleye fishing on Earth starts on Lake Erie in April and continues throughout the year. Meanwhile, while walleyes tend to hang closer to structure on inland waters until early summer, that's also when a percentage of the population starts suspending (swimming partway between bottom and surface). And that's when you can extend the principles of Erie's open-water trolling to anywhere in walleye country.

To start trolling for middle-of-nowhere walleyes on Erie—or anywhere else—you'll need some specialized gear, a motor that will troll down to slow speeds, and a willingness to wander in search of wandering walleyes. From there, successful open-water trolling depends to a large extent on speed control and just what constitutes the best potential water in the middle of nowhere. Even when you're 15 miles from shore on Lake Erie or Saginaw Bay, the smallest features make all the difference in the world.

Chairman of the Boards

For starters, gather up your planer boards and line-counter reels with matching rods. With boards you can pull everything from lightly weighted spinners and unweighted crankbaits to two ounces of weight with clip-on or in-line weights and even lead-core line.

For reels, set yourself up with quality line-counters. Distance of baits behind boards, we'll find out in a moment, is a crucial part of the equation. Next, team the reels with 8-foot to 8-foot, 6-inch rods with telescopic butt sections—stout enough to hold 3- to 4-ounce bottom bouncers off the boat without boards. The 8-foot, 6-incher has a softer tip that is perfect for trolling crankbaits and spinners with clip-on weights on boards. With its flex, it also helps keep big fish from coming unbuttoned. So does ten-pound monofilament, which incorporates some stretch into the picture but has plenty of toughness for landing monster walleyes.

Another key ingredient is a motor that allows you to troll at slow speeds. Whatever kind of motor it is—your big motor or an auxiliary kicker—it has to be able to troll down to slow speeds for Erie walleyes in spring. In the cold water of spring, it is essential to get your speed under 1 mph.

Seek and Strain

On the water, the first thing I rely on is my electronics. The two most important units in my boat are a color unit that spots fish in vibrant reds whether they're a few feet under the surface or pinned to the bottom and a GPS unit that allows me to monitor trolling speeds to tenths of a mile per hour and accommodates mapping cartridges. On the electronic maps I can see a wreck or a tiny bump in the bottom in the middle of nowhere and troll over it. When I catch or mark fish, I put out GPS waypoints so that I can return and work the same location time and again.

On Erie in spring, it's incredibly important to be able to mark fish and bait. Sometimes I run with my big motor at 25 mph just looking for schools, something not possible before the advent of modern fish finders. (**Tip:** Turn up the "ping" speed on the unit to help mark fish at high speeds.) I might cover a couple of miles of open water; when I mark clusters of fish, I punch in a waypoint and return later to fish them.

Nothing beats long, thin crankbaits for cold-water walleyes on the inland seas. My favorites are No. 10 and No. 12 Rapala Deep Down Husky Jerks. Most of the time I put them 30 to 80 feet behind the boards to reach 10 to 15 feet, the most productive depth level I've found. At times, though, the fish are even higher, in the top 5 feet, which necessitates putting out a Husky Jerk as little as 15 feet behind the board. I also like the No. 9 Rapala Tail Dancer 35 feet behind the board to keep the bait at 5 or 6 feet.

Since I'm trolling slowly, usually between 1.0 mph and 1.5 mph, I'm able to use spinners at the same time. Tie up some harnesses with #2 hooks and holographic spinner blades. I've lost far fewer fish on single hooks than on trebles, and holographics give off the right amount of flash to attract roaming walleyes from a distance. I weight them with a 1½-ounce bottom bouncer when open-water fishing, even though I'm nowhere near bottom. I'll have about a 6-foot leader between the spinner and the bouncer and then experiment with the distance behind the board from 20 to 40 feet, again covering similar depths of 8 to 18 feet. I put the bouncers on the inside boards and the cranks on the outside boards.

The best part of the system is that it's not just for Erie—or springtime—anymore. I use the same technique in summertime on inland lakes, but with higher-action cranks such as Storm Hot 'n' Tots and ThunderSticks and smaller (size 3) Northland blades. For weight I either stick with the bouncer or use clip-on weights to get the spinners down. Later in the year, though, it's a bit more difficult to fish cranks and spinners at the same time. Typically I stick with one presentation over the other, pulling cranks at 2.0 mph and spinners at 1.0 to 1.6 mph. Once again, look for fish and bait on the electronic and you're in business.

Trolling for walleyes in the middle of nowhere undoubtedly requires an attitude adjustment. Gone are the rock pinnacles and underwater castles that are so productive in many situations. Now is the time to start searching far and away from any underwater feature with electronics to find the fish and begin probing the water column with crankbaits and spinners. The fish are out there.

CHAPTER SEVEN

Early Options
on the Great Lakes

Fishing open water when there
are few alternatives.

Before spring on most inland waters, the options are anything but abundant. However, the abundance of the only option—the only game in town—is one of sheer plenitude. We're talking about the Great Lakes, from Michigan to Erie and beyond, where the waters around the river mouths are, with few exceptions, open year-round.

Which is why there's no time like the present to hit the couple of miles around rivers, reefs, and adjacent depths where walleyes will congregate in April. When covering water is at a premium and baitfish are in abundance—which is the rule, not the exception in the Great Lakes—trolling is the ticket not only to put a bait in front of more predators but also to stand out from the crowd of smelt, alewives, and gizzard shad. This is where the big ones live, often suspended over open water, feeding both day and night.

For numbers, there's always the opportunity to hit the reefs with jigs and mop up on smaller males. Seems to me the options are surprisingly varied for a time when, for all intents and purposes, nothing else is doing. Well, then again, not in my book…

Daytime Doings

In my early years, fishing with my grandfather and father in Michigan around the Muskegon Lake river mouth, we caught monster walleyes trolling near the beach and around the pier heads. The pattern still holds true, but since then I've found even greater numbers within a 2-mile radius of the river mouth. So it is from the Muskegon to Erie's Maumee.

During the day I start looking with electronics for bait and trolling for suspended fish that may be down 10 to 25 feet. Most of the time you'll see the bait, but unless the walleyes are highly concentrated, you'll seldom

Alewife is high on the list of walleye favorites. DAVID ROSE

see fish. Still, I put my lines out so that my crankbaits are running atop the schools of bait, since predators such as walleyes tend to look up, not down, when pursuing prey. When I spot a blob of bait on electronics that also have GPS capabilities, I punch in a waypoint or an icon for future reference. As I'm trolling I'll often identify four or five key schools of bait and then troll between them. Sometimes only one or two of the schools are holding walleyes. You have to cover water to find out.

Speed control and the proper lures are key to connecting. I troll with my 9.9-horsepower four-stroke kicker, which will push my big walleye boat at a slow crawl. My favorite speed during the daytime is about 1.5 mph. At this pace I get solid action out of Rapala Down Deep Husky Jerks, slim minnow baits that achieve excellent depth and have a light wobble that triggers fish in cold water. If I can't get the suspended fish going, or if I mark some big arcs near bottom, I'll switch over to lead core to get the cranks within a foot or two of bottom. But you have to watch the locator and pay close attention to the depth. The beauty of lead core is that if the

Smelt is one of the preferred forage species in the Great Lakes. DAVID ROSE

bottom rises, you simply speed up and the line lifts above the hump or ledge. When you get past it, count to 30 and then slow down. Lead core will sink back into the walleye's range.

On Erie, principles stay the same with bait and speed control, but I'll often troll the edges of reefs where the big females suspend. Planer boards are incredibly important to spread lines to the side, where fish scoot out when the boat goes over them. The walleyes simply move right into the path of the lures. In the popular areas of Erie off Niagara Reef or the Besse Davis Power Plant, I find most fish in the top 15 feet of the water column over 30-plus feet of water, which I reach with less than 50 feet of line behind boards.

Sometimes it's best to go especially slow, right around 1.0 mph. Such was the case when I took third in the 1999 *In-Fisherman* Professional Walleye Trail event out of Port Clinton. And while April's cold waters might be a little early for a crankbait with more wobble such as the Rapala Tail Dancer, the new balsa lures provide a touch more side-to-side movement to set your offering apart from the hordes of baitfish.

While the pinnacles of the reefs aren't the place to be for big fish, they're ideal for hordes of males that congregate there, waiting for the hens to move in. Again, keep an eye on your electronics, and when you see fish, get a jig down into them. Almost anything goes if it's a leadhead with a minnow. A little trick around a lot of small, aggressive walleyes is to put two minnows on the hook—the first one right side up, the second one upside down. This way, if one walleye filches your minnow, there's another on the hook in case the same fish comes back or another one moves in. The best depths I've found are from 8 to 15 feet.

After Hours

At night the waters come alive with even more monsters, which feed under the cover of darkness. The same trolling techniques are the way to go—moving from one baitfish pod to another—but it's important to make some adjustments. The reason: The fish do, too.

In darkness walleyes tend to move higher in the water column, up into the top 10 feet. Now is the time to switch from the gas kicker to a powerful trolling motor that has quality batteries and will ease along at 1.0 mph.

Now I can troll all night long with plenty of power. When I have tried trolling with the gas motor, I've caught fish the first few passes and then had them turn off because of the noise. With the electric motor, I keep catching them.

To work up higher toward the surface, I switch to No. 13 Original Rapalas on twenty-pound Berkley FireLine. Three No. 7 split-shots a few feet above it will get you down to 12 or 13 feet with 120 feet of line out. Remove a split-shot or let out less line to move higher. I seldom use planer boards at night, but if you must, keep small boards close to the boat, just beyond your other rods, to prevent congestion and bottlenecks with other trollers. Another reason to go without boards is the ability to pump the Rapala forward and drop it back—a key trigger. Slowly ease the rod forward about 18 inches, and drop it back on a tight line. I do this about twenty or thirty times a minute. Keep it gentle, otherwise you'll pull the lure away from too many walleyes, which miss when the bait has too much erratic action.

April is indeed a month of feast or famine. In other words, everything's doing on the Great Lakes. Now is the time to make your move.

You've waited, watched the TV weather, maybe even done a little "couch fishing" with a tackle box on your lap or a rod and reel in hand. But finally the wait is over. Will you hit it in the same spots at the same depths as last year? In other words, will you do the same old thing regardless of the weather? Sure, it's easy and reassuring to fish your memories—until you come up empty. That's why I find it more valuable to pay attention to the weather over the past few weeks and the conditions when the ice leaves. They're better clues to what's happening on your favorite waters than any recollections of years past. By paying attention to and considering how rapidly—or slowly—spring is arriving, you'll have a better idea of where and how to approach early-season walleyes.

SUMMER

CHAPTER EIGHT

Shades of Gray

Finer points of location and presentation.

Easy answers to fishing situations are just that—too easy. It's better to fill in the blanks when figuring out the ways of the walleye.

It's always tempting, whether tournament fishing or on a long vacation, to look for simple, black-and-white solutions to fishing conditions and where and how to catch walleyes as efficiently as possible. But shades of gray in response to the fish's reaction to weather, their shifting movements shallow or deeper, and their ever-changing moods are far more important. That's why, when there's a hot tip that the walleyes are chomping at whatever location and at whatever depth, it pays to take the time to figure out the details that make the walleyes' world go around. The shades of gray—the in-between areas of location and presentation that come with on-the-water interpretation—are what make the difference between following and leading the way to better fishing.

Bottom Bouncing

One of the best bets for summertime walleye angling is undoubtedly a bottom bouncer with a spinner. But when you get word that the fish are biting off a certain area at a specific depth, there's always more to it than that. Sure, it might be possible to catch fish at 20 to 25 feet for a day or two, but some particulars of the spot are going to be better than others, and the bite might not last through a change in the weather or a dip in the water temperature.

Well, what now? I know I have the right terminal tackle with bottom bouncers and spinners with holographic blades dressed with nightcrawlers. The slight adjustments in depth and to notice bottom content come next. If the wind blows, raising a chop, it's worthwhile to venture away from previously productive depths—say, 20 to 25 feet—to 10 or 15 feet. On the other hand, when the temperature drops, that's my cue to head deeper. Now I might search 28 to 35 feet.

When I'm searching, trying different depths, I always keep a sharp eye on color electronics, not only to mark fish but also to watch for pods of bait and bugs and to keep an eye out for hard bottom. Most times I find the

Walleye feed heavily on mayflies.
DAVID ROSE

active fish feeding on hard bottom; then, when I'm moving with a bottom bouncer and spinner, I try to find which direction the hard bottom runs and follow it shallow or deeper. By pulling the spinners over a wider area, you might wind up half a mile away from where you began, in an entirely new area that is far more productive than where you started. In essence, you now have an entirely new spot—something you wouldn't have if you had spent all your time in a limited stretch where rumor had it that the fish were biting. One trick when you mark a fish is to veer left or right to drag the spinner across the fish's face, a key triggering technique.

When you take cues from weather and electronics, it's much easier and much more probable that you'll be able to fill in the shades of gray. When you do, you'll find walleyes in a much broader area, where they'll keep biting today, tomorrow, and beyond.

Live-Bait Rigging

While dragging a leech or a nightcrawler on a slip-sinker rig seems the most straightforward recipe for success, the details of a spot's specifics, boat speed, and leader length are crucial ingredients that can mean the difference between dragging bait and fishing it efficiently.

When I inspect a spot with electronics, I look for hard bottom, transitions to soft bottom, and slight changes in depth that might concentrate walleyes. On a color liquid-crystal unit, the hard bottom will show in shades of yellow, red, or orange—more vibrant than over softer bottom. A slight dip of a foot or two might be all that's necessary to hold a pocket of walleyes.

The gray area between black-and-white bait presentation has to do with speed, boat control, and height above bottom with a rig. When rigging, it's very tempting to go too fast. As a result, I always try to cut my speed in half to let the bait go through its motions. (It might take me twenty minutes to cover a 20-yard stretch.) When I catch a fish, I punch an icon on my GPS to be able to return to the spot. On my way through the next time, I look for any cues that might have meant the fish-holding difference—the harder bottom, a cluster of rocks, a hatch of insects. When I move on to search for the next area, I raise the rig 2 to 3 feet off bottom, where the leader will be stretched out at the same level as the sinker. Often I find the fish willing to come up to take the bait. That in itself is an important differentiation—how high the walleyes are above bottom. (After all, a walleye will often rise a few feet to take a crankbait, and there's no difference here.) When I see a pattern with more fish biting with the bait off the bottom, that's a cue to repeat the pattern.

Much can be accomplished as well with variation in leader length. When I start prefishing for a tournament or fun fishing with friends and we're rigging with bait, we all start with different leader lengths. Vary the lengths between 2 feet and as long as 8 to 10 feet, and note when the longer leader gets bit—your cue to work the bait above bottom.

Again, watch your electronics for any details and for the height of the walleyes off bottom, which can mean the difference between dragging bait underneath the fish and putting it in their faces.

Crankbait Casting

Ready to fill in the shades of gray with a faster, more run-and-gun attack? Well, it's possible when you notice the details around you. In shallow water, where crankbait casting excels, I'm always looking for something different—a pocket in the weeds, brush, or a slight change in depth, even if it's just a foot or two.

Electronics are often every bit as important in depths of 5 feet or less as in 25 feet. The reason is that with a quality locator, it's possible to ease into a shallow clog of weeds and then back out just a touch to the edges, where walleyes occupy the feeding lanes. Another key is wearing quality polarized sunglasses to see the lanes, clumps, and openings. With my Solar Bat sunglasses, I can see dark spots beneath the water, indicating weeds and open lanes where fish travel and feed.

But I don't get stuck in a rut just fishing the edges or with the same lures or colors. If the wind blows, it's another cue to move into water as shallow as 2 feet. Meanwhile, I like to have a partner cast to the water beyond the weeds to find out if the fish are beyond them. You don't need to get hung up on one kind of weeds over another. Although I like cabbage weeds in the shallows as much as the next guy, coontail or even stringy weeds will still hold bait and, therefore, walleyes. When I'm working an area hard with No. 5 Rapala Shad Raps—a great bait for casting atop and

around weed edges—I change colors each time I make a pass through the area. One time I might try a rattling RS Shad Rap, and the next time a jointed version. If you're simply looking for black-and-white solutions and keep on throwing the same color, you're probably going to miss out on more bites that you could have caught.

Another thing I try to do is fish an entire area and not just focus on the key spots. With wind, for instance, the fish might reposition themselves or work farther downwind to where bait often collects with the currents. Go ahead and fish a longer stretch to find more spots scattered throughout the area before going back to the well one more time. In windy conditions I couldn't fish without powerful, long-lasting deep-cycle batteries, which hold their energy all day long, even in high winds. Recently, in a tournament on Devils Lake in North Dakota, I was able to keep fishing windblown shallows when other competitors had dead batteries and were relying on their outboard motors to position their boats.

While we all like easy answers to any fishing situation, what's more important is figuring out what the fish are doing from day to day and even hour to hour. Sure, the black-and-white approach is a starting point. The shades of gray, however, will mean more walleyes—not only when conditions change but also when you expand your thinking to explore all the possibilities.

Opposite: Old docks and pilings next to deep water are tried-and-true walleye hangouts. DAVID ROSE

CHAPTER NINE

Summer Highs and Lows

Cruising up top or lying down low, the walleyes are where you— and your electronics—find them.

Summertime in walleye country is a time of highs and lows. Sure, some folks complain about the fishing during the dog days—that would be a low point—but I look at highs and lows not in terms of how the fish are biting but in regard to the fish's position in the water column. That's because a bunch of fish could be clustered on bottom, and a separate population is probably going to be suspended partway down over the lake's deep water. You had better be ready for the highs and lows.

That's why, whenever I launch my boat on a Midwest lake with a decent walleye population, the first thing I do is go looking with electronics. I look around deepwater structure—points, humps, ridges—for the telltale marks of bait and the fish that are in the area to feed on them. But sometimes the

Running in search of walleye with the kicker motor next to the Mercury Verado. DAVID ROSE

depths look like the Serengeti, devoid of life. My next move is to idle over the deep water in the neighborhood, looking for baitfish and, sometimes, walleyes. Since many of the walleyes scoot out from the boat's path, you aren't going to mark them. The bait in itself, however, is an indication to start fishing the open water. When you're ready for both options, be prepared for the highs and lows—it won't be long before you stop dogging the dog days.

Reach Deep

For starters, take a look at quality maps of wherever you're fishing. On them you'll see the lake's most prominent points and biggest humps. I like the ones that go into the deepest water available. Depending on the lake, "deep" could be anywhere from 30 to 80 feet. Whichever it is, you're on the right track.

Although the temptation is to drop lines down immediately, I suggest spending an hour with your electronics. For down-deep bottom fish, color electronics are an incredible advantage, and in the past couple of years, I've learned a lot from the new generation of locators. While searching some of my favorite spots from over the years, I've found that the top feeding areas are where the lake basin goes from soft (usually a dark blue on the color locators) to hard, which is shown in a more intense signal of yellow and orange. That's where you want to be, fishing the transitions between soft and hard.

The most efficient way I know to cover that transition area and to find more via your own sense of feel is with a bottom bouncer and a spinner. A good guideline for weight is an ounce for every 10 feet of water. A 3-ounce bottom bouncer is therefore most effective in the 30-foot range. About 4 feet behind the bouncer, I use a spinner with a nightcrawler or, when nipping perch are a bother, an artificial nightcrawler. I always run my bouncers on baitcasting tackle and with a casting reel spooled with twenty-pound Berkley FireLine, a no-stretch superline that gives you the ability to feel rocks that might hold fish. But when you drop a bouncer down to bottom, it's best not to drag it. Keep your trolling motor at a speed fast enough to make the spinner's blade rotate, and then touch bottom with the weight's wire feeler, lift off bottom, and periodically touch bottom to make sure you're in the zone. That's why I like to call the technique "bottom testing" instead of bottom bouncing.

Suspended Animation

Often, though, the fish won't be pinned to bottom. You're going to have to make a judgment call based on where you're fishing. Are there enough fish on the bottom to make bouncing worthwhile? If I'm not marking dozens over a decent-size stretch, I'm not fishing them.

That's your signal to break out the planer boards and start trolling. Another signal has to do with what you can see with a good pair of polarized sunglasses. With the glasses I wear, I often see schools of minnows darting around midlake, just under the surface. It's a sign that suspended fish aren't far below.

After I start up my Mercury kicker motor, I'm going to start trolling a selection of crankbaits in the heart of summer. I like to keep my speed at 1.6 to 2.2 mph on GPS—a good range for catching walleyes. To give the fish a selection of baits at varying heights, I'll start with a Storm Hot 'n' Tot 40 feet back and a No. 7 Rapala Tail Dancer 100 feet back to target 9 and 11 feet,

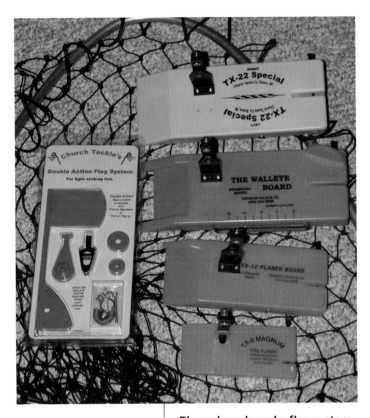

Planer boards and a flag system are the tools of the open-water trollers when running multiple lines. DAVID ROSE

respectively, when I clip on planer boards to swing them out to the side of the boat. While those are my outside boards, I'll weight another Tail Dancer with a 1-ounce clip-on weight at 50–50 (meaning, 50 feet out, clip on a 1-ounce weight, let out 50 more feet, and clip on the board) to get a little deeper, into the low teens. Another excellent combination to dig deeper is with a No. 5 Rapala Jointed Shad Rap (I love the blue with the orange belly). I let out 50 feet and then clip on a 2- or 3-ounce weight that then goes 20 to 35 behind the board. This gets well into the teens. Now you've got a range of depths covered with a range of lures. When one lure starts to get action, it's a signal to move two or more to the same level with the same lure selection.

Highs and lows are a fact of life for summer walleyes. Electronics will give an idea of which extreme it's going to be.

CHAPTER TEN

Going for a Troll

Effective trolling = location, depth, speed, and lure action.

Summer is a fine time to troll. The water has warmed, boosting the walleyes' activity level. The fish have long since dispersed from spawning grounds, their tails taking them to a variety of locations around the lake. And the regulations in most states allow multiple lines per person, giving you the opportunity to experiment with running depth, color, and lure shape and size. Indeed, now is the time to go for a troll.

The way I look at it, trolling is best for focusing on a couple of general locations. One is the edge of structure; the other is open water. In each instance you'll need to take into account trolling speed, depth, and the lure actions that make the most sense given the season. Here's how to tip the odds in your favor.

Crank Yankers

When I'm trolling the edges of structure, I like to search with crankbaits on Berkley FireLine. Together, between the lures and line, you have the right combination to pull free from weeds and monitor your line should you not be able to shed the pesky grass. It's better to be able to tell if a lure is fouled and then reel it in than to troll it unproductively with a clump of grass decorating it.

If I'm dealing with a flat or a long point, I find the general depth at which the bottom peaks. If the point has a primary depth of 12 feet, I'm going to try to run my crankbaits above that level. How to do it? I start by staggering the amount of FireLine I have out. I also like to run four of the same style of bait, enabling me to achieve different running depths to figure out where the walleye are located in the water column. I might run four Rapala Jointed Shad Raps, one back 20 feet, another back 40 feet, and—when I have a partner with me in a two-rod state—the next two at 60 and 80 feet. If that doesn't get the fish going, next time I'll stagger them back 30, 50, 70, and 90 feet.

I'll put two of the small cranks on planer boards that I can read when the crank fouls in weeds. The other two rods I'll put in rod holders back by the transom. I'll often run them without boards, and I'm able to see the rod tips vibrate due to the sensitive twenty-pound FireLine (same diameter as eight-pound monofilament). If the lures pick up debris, I'm often able to pick up the rod, give it a good rip, and clean the bait—you'll be able to feel it running free and wobbling once again.

For speeds with the crankbaits and much more, I look at my combo fish finder/GPS unit. I'm able to put the unit on split screen, with the finder operating on one side and the GPS on the other. Making the most of the combo unit, I can repeat my plot trail over a productive stretch or deviate from it slightly to cover a fresh swath of water. Meanwhile, for most cranking, motoring with a 9.9-horsepower kicker motor, I'll vary my speed between 1.6 mph and 2.2 mph—a range that can be adjusted by tenths of a mile per hour according to the GPS unit. If I don't get the fish going on the jointed Shad Raps, I'll switch to four Storm Hot 'n' Tots of the same size, or maybe four Rapala Tail Dancers.

Mmmm, Crawlers...

What about fish that are in the middle of the lake? Yes, crankbaits are great, but trolling with spinners and nightcrawlers is a technique that works everywhere from open water on Saginaw Bay, in my home state of Michigan, to the little lake nearest you.

Here's the deal: Once water temperatures get into the 70s, a common pattern throughout walleye country is for fish to suspend. Spinners are a good deal because you can run them slowly, in the 1.0-mph range, and stay in the fish zone longer.

On small inland waters you can just idle around the middle of the lake, looking for bait and predators on electronics. On much larger waters, such as Saginaw Bay or Lake Erie, I'll use the contour maps displayed on my electronics to look for underwater points and humps. Or I'll run contour lines at a given depth by looking at the mapping display.

Lately, rather than weighting spinners with clip-on weights with the 50–50 method—that is, 50 feet between spinner and weight and another 50 feet between weight and board—I'll pick 1- or 2-ounce weights, depending on the depth, and run equal leader lengths between spinner and weight (either 30 or 40 feet). Next I'll run the weights in staggered distances behind the boards—say, 10, 20, 30, and 40 feet.

Around the Great Lakes' monster walleyes, I adjust the sizes of my spinners, choosing a minimum size of a #4 blade, often preferring #5s. Check out a variety of holographic blades, as well as painted blades and the always excellent hammered copper, silver, and gold. Inland I'll go with #3s and #4s most of the time. Also, with spinners I like to go with monofilament for its stretch, which allows a light-biting walleye to get the hooks in its mouth and keep it from coming unbuttoned. Ten-pound is a favorite.

Well, why not go for a troll? The time is right. The fish are dispersed, and their activity level is gaining momentum with the coming of summer. Get them while the getting's good.

Opposite: I like to set my trolling rods before I get to my GPS waypoint. DAVID ROSE

CHAPTER ELEVEN

Slip-Bobber Secrets

How to fish with bobbers for specificity.

At times, no way of catching walleyes is more effective than the simple, stealthy slip-bobber. In my book, bobbers (aka floats) aren't rock 'em, sock 'em exciting like casting crankbaits at night or pitching jigs shallow to wrestle up giant walleyes, but the deadly precision of a float with a jig and lively bait is often what it takes to put fish in the box. And sometimes the bobber does it better than anything else in your repertoire.

Summer is one of those times—when walleyes gang up on the tips of points, on flats, on the edges of rocks, and on and around other underwater features. With electronics and an underwater camera, it's possible to take bobber fishing to a new level by spotting the height of the walleyes (and making sure that the fish you're marking are walleyes) and then zeroing in on them. Bobbers also excel when insect hatches begin, clouding the water with scads of bugs for the walleyes to eat. At such times the walleyes spurn every crawler you put past them—until a small leech suspended below a float is just what the Bobber Doctor ordered.

Scope 'Em Out

Nothing beats specificity when picking the best places for bobbering. That means I'm looking for specific points and turns and bottom content. The more precise, the better. The reason is that bobbering is such a slow-go technique—when bobbering, you cover a fraction of the water that trolling would sift or casting would strain.

When I'm checking a point, I want to find the area where the deepest water swings in next to it, or where a patch of weeds is growing off the tip. Another example is a forest on places like Devils Lake, North Dakota. There, in a lake with a ton of flooded timber, the best areas are where I can find a drop-off of as little of 2 feet within the trees. That is often enough to concentrate the walleyes big-time.

Many times, if I'm faced with tough fish, particularly those suspended off bottom on tight structure, I'll rely on both my liquid-crystal locators—bowmount and transom mount—and my underwater camera. With the fish finders I'm able to note the presence of fish and bait. Then I drop down the camera to see what kind of fish I'm marking—and which ones are at which height off bottom. On points in natural lakes throughout the Midwest, I've seen the walleyes at one level and the crappies right above them. Since you want to put your leeches at the walleye's level, not the crappie's, the camera is indispensable for pinpointing the level at which to place your bait.

Lively Leeches

Which brings us to the bobber rig. When I set up a bobber rig, I rely on a rod of at least 7 feet—the better to sweep slack out of the line and set hooks. Another great way to eliminate slack (and know the whereabouts of your bobber) is to fill your reel with four- or six-pound high-visibility monofilament line, a bright green that's easy to see when the bobber is away from the boat. Then I tie a ball-bearing snap swivel to the end of the main line and add a 3-foot leader of fluorocarbon. The fluoro, of course, provides an invisible leader, and the swivel keeps the bobber from sliding up against a fish when you're reeling it in. The bobber goes above the

Leeches are prime forage for summertime walleye. Northland Gum Drop floaters help suspend the bait off the bottom while rigging. DAVID ROSE

swivel, with a rubber or cloth bobber stop that slides easily through the rod's guides.

The other end of the rig is of crucial importance. My favorite bait for any bobber rig is a leech—a very lively one, since the angler gives it very little action. The leech has to do all the work itself, with a little inspiration from the wind. That's why I depend on a polyester mesh bag. The bag, with a Velcro seal atop it, goes in your live or bait well with leeches in it. The bag lets the leeches swim and scrape themselves of crud that would otherwise suffocate and kill them. When you reach into the carrier, the leeches practically jump out of your hand—perfect for bobbering.

At the business end of the fluorocarbon, I like to put a jig for color and weight. Of all the jig styles, I prefer a vertically oriented jig. My next choice is a ballhead jig. The vertically oriented jig hangs straight up and down in the water, and if you can find jigs equipped with No. 4 Kahle hooks, you get efficient hookups. Just hook the leech behind the suction cup, and you're in business.

When the bobber goes down, take advantage of the mint line to reel up all the slack until you feel the fish on the tip of the rod. Next go for a big, sweeping hookset, and reel like a madman to wind out any remaining slack. Fish on!

That, of course, is precisely the goal of summertime fishing—fishing anytime, really. Bobbers and a lively leech will do the job when the walleyes are packed up on precise spots.

CHAPTER TWELVE

Bounce with an Ounce (or Two or Three)

When, where, and how bottom and bouncing unite.

Make no mistake, the ingenious bottom bouncer, a lead weight with an R-shaped arm and wire feeler, has midsummer magic in it. In sum, it gets a bait—be it a spinner, a crawler ahead of a bead, even a floating Rapala—down to bottom and keeps it there at a walleye's preferred speed (which is to say, slow). What's more, walleyes gravitate to deep water when it's warm out, and that's where bottom and bouncing unite.

The first step, of course, is searching with electronics. The next steps: marking 'em and mowing 'em down with a combination of artificial intelligence and live bait acumen.

Find 'Em First

Enter the utility of high-powered modern electronics. A case in point is the new generation of color units, which pair a wide-screen liquid-crystal unit of more than 11 diagonal inches with GPS technology. For starters, crank up the sensitivity to around 90 percent, far less than the "maximum" level needed on earlier black-and-white models. High sensitivity can pose a tricky learning curve, since you'll register a lot of interference, including air bubbles, but fish will stand out as colored arcs, partial arcs, blobs, and clusters in reds and oranges. (Color helps separate fish from bottom.) Beyond looking for fish, watch for bait.

Walleyes, after all, are never far from their food. Even if you're marking bait without fish, their presence probably indicates the level of the walleyes, and you can pull a spinner rig at their depth or look in other spots around the lake at the same depth, perhaps 22 feet. Whatever it is, it gives you a starting point.

Lead, Leader, and More

Start the search by pulling bouncers and spinners over spots where you see fish on electronics. To determine if they're walleyes, you have a couple of options: One is an underwater camera; the other is fishing for them (yep, you'll know when you catch one).

Working spinner and bouncers, though, takes some know-how. Foremost is how much weight to use. I like bottom bouncers with a bend in them—not an eyelet for connecting line—for their solid wire construction, variety of weights to 4 ounces, and the option of painted lead (in walleye-favorite colors of chartreuse and lime as well as chartreuse and orange). A good guideline to use is an ounce of weight for every 10 feet of depth. Hence, if I'm working 20 feet I'm going to want a 2-ounce bouncer; if I'm working 30 feet, I want a 3-ouncer.

Another consideration is leader length. When there are a lot of snags, such as rocks or wood, I shorten my spinner's leaders to 2½ to 3 feet. If the bottom's clean and the water clear, I extend the leader to 4 or 5 feet.

For a rod and reel, I wouldn't consider pulling a bouncer without a baitcaster. A good choice is a 6-foot, 6-inch baitcaster. Take a small

baitcasting reel, fill it with fourteen- or twenty-pound Berkley FireLine, and you're in business. Know that a smallish baitcaster is more comfortable to hold.

Blade Runners

When you're marking fish or their foodstuffs, take the appropriate bouncer and a spinner behind it. On inland waters I will use a No. 2 to No. 3 blade most of the time. (Northland has some excellent holographic blades of such sizes on pretied rigs 60 inches long; snip 'em shorter if you need to go around snags.) If there are juvenile perch in your lake, try the green blade with gold on the concave side. Painted chartreuse blades, often found in bulk bins, are excellent in clear water. So, too, are the holographic rainbow blades.

The next key is speed. More than anything else, such as watching GPS speeds, I'll gauge my speed visually by turning up my bowmount trolling motor just fast enough to make the blade spin.

In addition to monitoring your speed, you're going to want to keep the bouncer near to but not dredging bottom. In fact, a more accurate term than bottom bouncing is "bottom testing." At the right speed to make the blade spin, let out line until the bouncer ticks bottom, then lift it up 6 inches or so. Drop it back to test for bottom every twenty or thirty seconds. Watch your electronics, too, to help you anticipate when to lift the bouncer over a rise in bottom or when to let it back with a slight dip. It's also helpful to keep your rig at a 45-degree angle behind the boat. When you have more line out and a greater angle, that's too much. You need either less line or more weight.

Another thing I'll try is an Aberdeen hook—a No. 4, for instance— with a bead and half crawler. I'll also go with a heavier weight and kick up the speed above 1.0 mph and put a Original Rapala on a 4-foot lead. Start with something small, maybe a No. 7 or a No. 9, again in a color that matches the lake's forage—perch, for instance.

Indeed, the bouncer is a midsummer's dream. It gets down to bottom at nice, slow speeds. It stays there when you manage your line at a 45-degree angle. That's when, where, and how bottom and bouncing unite.

CHAPTER THIRTEEN

A River Runs Through It

A reservoir is like a river in both high times and low.

In essence, a reservoir is a river—a bottled-up river, to be precise. With a dam at the downstream end to harness power or to create upstream habitat, a reservoir nevertheless runs like a river, with current from the original source flowing through the impoundment. That's why, to understand and to fish a reservoir more effectively for walleyes, it helps to start thinking of an impoundment more like moving water than a static system.

Whenever I approach a reservoir, I focus for starters on the original creek channel, the source of current and flow on any impoundment. In a way, the main creek channel, as well as adjoining feeder channels, is like an aquatic highway, providing a thoroughfare for fish to travel. Next I analyze current water conditions—whether the water is rising or falling. If a reservoir is swelling with rain or shriveling from drought, walleyes will respond in predictable fashion, moving shallow when the water is high and retreating to the depth of the channels when low. By reading a reservoir as

To find walleye in a reservoir, like Kentucky's Lake Cumberland, fish as you would if it were moving water. DAVID ROSE

if it were a river, I'm able to stick with the fish through thick and thin—or, I should say, high and low.

How Low Will It Go?

Sadly, low water is the rule, not the exception, on most reservoirs throughout the walleye belt. Most notably, the Dakota reservoirs are currently at all-time lows. Spots I once fished in 20 feet of water are now high and dry.

To pattern summertime fish on reservoirs with low water, I immediately seek out the river channel and points where the channel swings in. The best way to find the spots where the river turns and reaches near shore and tapering points is on a quality map that quickly gives me the whereabouts of the channel and the points.

While a point is always an excellent place to start fishing, it's possible the point will be clear out of the water in times of drought, which is why I also look for bends in the river channel and places where creeks intersect the channel. Bends and places where creeks meet are going to be located in some of the deepest water in the reservoir—the place to go for summertime walleyes in low water. (Flooded timber is a bonus, too.) This pattern has remarkable similarity to fishing a river in low water, where you look for the deepest holes and pockets.

If, on the other hand, the water is rising, it's time to check the back bays and the points at the mouths of them. As I would in a river, I look for points with hard bottom. On electronics, any little transition from softer bottom to hard bottom—perhaps clay or gravel—will key walleye location. In sum, head for the creeks when the water's high; retreat for the channels when it's low.

No matter what the water is doing, I always keep in mind the direction of the current and start fishing the upstream side, which is where the most active fish will position themselves. When jigging, I also know to fish downstream with a jig, slipping with the current whenever possible. An exception is when trolling, when it's most effective to troll upstream with crankbaits.

Search and Stealth

For finding fish in reservoirs, no setup is more effective than a bottom bouncer trailed by a spinner with a nightcrawler. In deeper water I count on an ounce of weight for every 10 feet of depth. In the shallows, when the water is less than 10 feet deep, I'll often go light with a ¼-ounce bouncer ahead of my spinner. Once again, it all depends on whether the water is high or low and the fish are, therefore, shallow or deep. One reason spinners are so effective is that the stretches of creek channel you'll be working—or points and bluffs, for that matter—are often 1,000 yards long, which would take forever to fish with a jig or a live-bait rig. Another excellent search tool is a crankbait, a No. 5 Rapala Shad Rap on twenty-pound Berkley FireLine. Troll it upstream to tick bottom about half the time. Knocking bottom is an effective triggering technique, and by covering water you'll find fish you can return to later with a jig and an extra measure of precision. (If a lot of wood litters the bottom, I'll replace my crankbait's trebles with weedless hooks to reduce snags and lost lures.)

For fishing more precisely once you've located key stretches of channel or points, switch to a jig—a rattle jig, in fact, is my top choice. No place is a rattle jig more effective than on reservoirs stirred by wind and current.

Six- or eight-pound flame Berkley FireLine is the way to go for its high visibility when jigging and for the extra shake and rattle you can impart to a jig with the stretch-free line. In reservoirs I'll often start with a soft plastic tail before trying live bait. For bait, it's hard to beat either a fathead minnow or a half nightcrawler. If I find deep water with logs, I'll vertically jig in the limbs, shaking the bait to give it motion and sound.

Opposite: David Rose pulls in a sauger. MARK MARTIN

When the Going Gets Tough...

What to do when reservoir bite is brutal? That's when I seek out saugers, a blotchy cousin of the walleye. Saugers in reservoirs are incredibly aggressive, smacking jigs fished vertically or on three-way rigs pulled upstream. When scouting for saugers, I look for the deepest water in the reservoir, often 40 to 60 feet deep. I'll bulk up with big jighead as heavy as ¾ ounce, which saugers love. Saugers also love plastic curly tails. If I'm fishing a three-way rig, I put a big jig with a plastic tail on an 8-inch dropper off the three-way swivel and tie a floating jighead with a minnow onto a trailing line about 2 feet long. Then I ease upstream with my bowmount electric, watching my electronics for signs of life below.

If you mark saugers, you're going to catch them. Often it's helpful to take a little extra time to scout the deep water before starting to fish. If you do, saugers will often save the day. Combine the sauger's unabashed aggressiveness with the principles of high and low water, and a reservoir becomes a much less mysterious place. Read it like a river, and you'll be able to prevail through the highs and lows.

CHAPTER FOURTEEN

Alive and Lively

When reality bites and live bait makes sense.

When the going gets tough, the tough get baiting. At least that's the way I look at it when faced with adverse conditions in the realm of the walleye. Sudden weather changes, fishing pressure, and factors unbeknownst to us humans can all put fish off their feed. Enter the great equalizer—live bait.

So many times, in both fun and tournament fishing, I've seen no better way to pluck fish than with the liveliest bait presented with a measure of stealth and precision. It's a technique that works spring to fall, whenever cold fronts roll in or a pack of boats sours the walleye's mood. The trick is to stay over the fish with electronics, check their exact position with an underwater camera, and then mop up with a gentle touch.

A leech tamer bag like this one keeps leeches lively. DAVID ROSE

The Place for Bait

I always start with the best bait I can find, and perhaps my favorite is a lively leech. Leeches deter pecking panfish, won't tear like crawlers, and absolutely do a number on walleyes. But you have to take care of them. Even after weeks in my live well, leeches stay active and energetic with the help of a mesh bag that not only lets the critters acclimate to the temperature of the lake but also allows them to scrub themselves clean and keeps them from suffocating (which they frequently do in a foam cup or plastic container). When I reach for one, it's jamming. And it's going to catch me more walleyes.

Crawlers are also an excellent summertime offering. (Since there's nothing akin to a mesh bag for crawlers, you're just going to have to keep them cold to keep them in top condition.) Inject your crawler with just a bit of air, otherwise you'll end up with an enormous sausage of a worm that will float too high off bottom. A touch of air will keep the crawler down

Caching crawlers in Styrofoam boxes keeps them active especially in warm weather.
DAVID ROSE

in the fish zone. Keep an eye on your electronics to determine how high the fish are from bottom and how high in relation you want to run your crawler.

Now I put my bait in a place where I know there are fish, either from experience over the past few days or with the aid of my electronics. Say you've fished for a few days with bottom bouncers and spinners and cleaned up on walleyes before the bite goes south. I move in to the same areas with a live-bait rig with a sliding sinker and a long snell of 6 to 12 feet, and let the bait do its thing. The best way to present it is by moving with the wind, controlling the drift with an electric motor, and letting the leech (or crawler) jam and jive. The walleyes are going to take the bait. If I don't have a history in the area, I study structure with my color electronics to find the walleyes' whereabouts.

Another tack is to use an underwater camera. While it's possible to work an area and catch a fish here or there, I'll drop my camera to actually see why I've found the walleyes in a particular place. Sometimes you'll see walleyes relating to low-lying weeds, or perhaps rocks. When you know such information, it's easy to repeat the successful pattern by finding similar areas.

It's also possible to find out if the fish are atop the structure—say, a point or reef—and then duplicate what you've learned in the next spot. Typically I find that walleyes are down at the base of the structure, often on the transition from hard to soft bottom, unless the wind's howling. Then they often move atop it.

At a time like this you can often look for the edge of shallow breaks with the naked eye—well, at least with a pair of quality polarized sunglasses. Quality polarized glasses are just the ticket for spotting edges of breaks, shallow rocks, even fish. On clear waters, even in wind, it's possible to spot walleyes cruising the shallows. This is a time to toss a lively bait in there on a light slip-sinker rig or with a split-shot.

Tackling Up

One of the most crucial elements to fishing bait the right way is proper tackle and technique. As I grow older (dare I say wiser?), I've lightened up my spinning tackle to feel bites and to tease walleyes into taking. Where I once used a medium-action rod for live-bait rigging, I've switched to a medium-light rod. And while I once used tiny hooks, as small as No. 8, I now seldom go smaller than a No. 4.

Why the changes? Medium-light graphite rods have the ability to sense light bites and to "weigh up" fish. By that I mean it's possible to feed line to a fish when you sense a bite, and then tighten up a touch to a point where the walleye bends the rod a bit. This indicates whether a fish (and not a rock) has a hold of the bait and lets me tighten up before setting the hook. It helps, meanwhile, to have a sharp and wide-gapped hook such as a No. 4 octopus—red hooks that often seem to make a difference for their color and attraction when fishing bait.

One final piece of vital equipment is a powerful set of trolling motor batteries. Long life on the water is precisely what you'll need when battling waves or other adverse conditions. From there, with the boat in position, the rest is up to you—and your bait.

CHAPTER FIFTEEN

When Opportunity Knocks

There's nothing but possibility in all depths on the transition out of summer.

For midsummer walleyes, there's nothing but possibilities—for both you and the fish. At a time of year when they might be located anywhere from 4 to 40 feet of water, you had best explore every option. That means shallow, deep, and even the space between. But I always have a starting point to get the day under way and go from there...

Down Deep

When the waters warm, I know to expect fish in deep water, and the fastest way to find them is with the combination of maps and electronics. Wherever I'm fishing, I look to a state fisheries agency, U.S. Coast Guard, or other hydrographic contour map to narrow the search. I use them to check for the most prominent structures, including humps and points, adjacent to deep water. Those are almost always the best places to begin.

When you're on the water, motor around the structure and the nearby deep water, watching on electronics for baitfish and accompanying predators. Remember, you've spent good money on a fish locator, so it makes sense to use it to locate fish before you start fishing. On the new color units, it's possible to see the finest of detail—bugs, bait, and even fish glued to the bottom. Use them to narrow your search. If you're wondering exactly what you're marking, drop down an underwater camera to have a look. At times I've found that the fish I'm seeing on a locator are walleyes; other times I've seen less desirable species on which I'd rather not waste my time.

After you've found a level where the walleyes are holding, I know of no more effective way to trigger them than with a bottom bouncer and spinner. When I'm up front in my boat, running my bowmount electric trolling motor, I drop down two bouncer rigs. I hand-hold one and put the other in a rod holder. For terminal tackle, my top choices are bottom bouncers and spinner rigs, particularly those with blades in the new holographic shades. A good guideline for bouncer weight is an ounce for every 10 feet of water—1 ounce in 10 feet, 2 ounces in 20, and so forth. On the spinners, nothing beats a nightcrawler, except possibly when panfish are on the attack, which is when I switch to plastic to beat back the little rascals. Simply ease around with the trolling motor at speeds between 0.5 and 1.2 mph, and it shouldn't be long until you get the fish to go. But in case you don't…

Try Shallow

When I don't find walleyes deep, the next place I go is the shallows, where I look for cover in the form of weeds and brush. There I pitch jigs with a leech or half a nightcrawler in pockets and holes between the obstructions. Look for hard bottom within the weeds, which concentrates walleyes. I still use a flasher-style fish finder—a seemingly old-fashioned locator—to find hard bottom. Then I stick with those patches of bottom until I find fish.

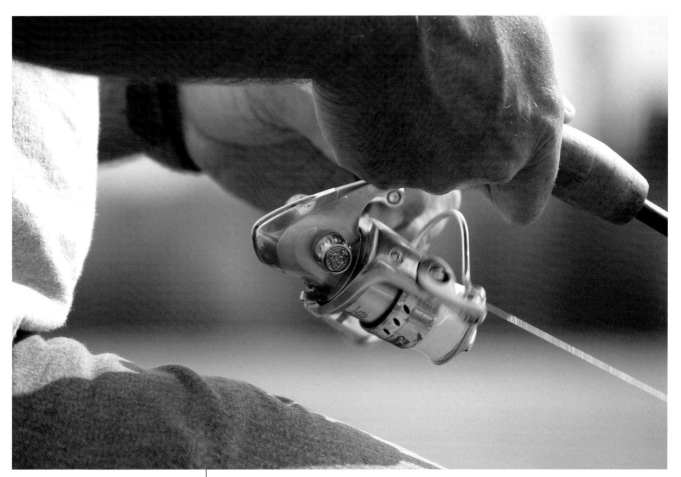

This reel is filled with flame-green FireLine. DAVID ROSE

To fish through the weedy, brushy difficulties, I like a weedless jig, with its sleek shape and plastic weed guards to help slide through without snagging. You'll get more hookups if you soften the plastic by bending it back and forth. Usually, when you're pitching pockets you don't have to fish a jig in there for long—toss it in, twitch it a few times, reel it in, and do it again. The reason is that weed fish are normally aggressive and will hit within moments of spotting the bait—often on the initial fall. So watch your line closely for a twitch or for a move off to the side. You can't beat highly visible flame Berkley FireLine for just such reasons, to say nothing of its strength in pulling free from weeds or wrestling out a walleye. But when the weed fish aren't going…

Move In Between

That's when I go to the midrange—the space between the shallows and the deep. There, again, I look with electronics for baitfish or suspended fish. The fastest way to search is with crankbaits behind planer boards. The reason is that you can pull crankbaits from 2.0 to 3.0 mph—far faster than the 1.0-mph speed with spinners and nightcrawlers.

The best summertime lures are ones with action—ones that have a more distinct wobble than you'd use in spring. Now I turn to jointed Rapala Shad Raps and Tail Dancers behind planer boards. Match the Raps to the water color—natural patterns in clear water, brighter shades and firetigers in darker. I'll stagger the crankbaits to reach high in the water column and at moderate depths, depending on where I'm seeing fish. But even when fish are in short supply on the electronics, I'll work the area, since walleyes often scoot out to the sides of the boat when it passes over. This is the perfect scenario for trolling with boards—the boat pushes fish out into the path of your lures.

Deep, shallow, and everywhere in between… Yep, you've got to do what you've got to do in summertime. Between all the options, you're bound to get bit.

FALL

CHAPTER SIXTEEN

Shallow to Deep

Finding walleyes in as little as a few inches of water to as deep as 80 feet.

In fall, walleyes can be anywhere—6 inches under the surface in 80 feet of water or tight to bottom in 10 feet. Sound challenging? It can be, unless you know how walleyes drift off structure and suspend in the vicinity of bait. Finding them is a looking game with quality electronics; catching them is a straining game with planer boards, spinners, and crankbaits. The pattern holds true wherever you are, from the Great Lakes to inland waters, and wherever walleyes are chasing baitfish. Which, it turns out, is everywhere.

The Baiting Game

The bait connection betrays the walleye's presence. In fall, when walleyes ramp up their feeding before winter, the fish will never be far from food. On the Great Lakes you might see enormous pods of 1- to 3-inch gizzard shad skittering on the surface or as big blobs on a locator. Shiners and the like also herd up on inland waters, and predators are never far behind.

How do you find them? Start looking for structure on a map and then with electronics. Points, humps, and weed edges are all fair game. But when you look with a quality locator that pinpoints fish and bait, the key is to veer away from the structure and look over open water. If you've seen fish on structure at a certain level—15 feet, for instance—you can bet they'll be at that same depth over open water, from hundreds of yards to half a mile away from the structure. Walleyes will do this day and night. The most important thing to remember is not to glue yourself to structure—the walleyes will wander away from it if bait is present in open water.

Search Mode

The best way to enter into search mode is to start trolling. This way you can cover water and zigzag to find fish. It would be far too time-consuming to jig or live-bait your rig. Trolling, on the other hand, spreads lines to the sides of the boat and behind it—the better to cover a swath of water at different depths.

I always try to maximize my efforts with the most rods possible and the greatest coverage. Enter planer boards, the handy devices that veer lines away from the boat. With them you can run more rods without tangling and pull lures through more territory.

Which brings us to my two favorite offerings in fall. While few people fish spinners after summertime, the reliable crawler harness keeps working through October and even into November. You can boost up a size or two with your spinners in fall to tempt more big fish. If, for instance, you were using No. 2 blades in summer, you now might want to try 4s and 5s. The heavier thrum is often just what the walleyes want when they're starting to feed with gusto before winter. And since baitfish, more than bugs, are the main course of fall walleyes, try holographic blades in silver shiner, gold shiner, golden perch, and other colors to mimic baitfish.

By November, though, I normally start switching to crankbaits. You can move them faster and cover more water (2.0 or 2.3 mph for cranks versus 1.1 mph for crawlers), and since the fish are so keyed on baitfish, cranks will often do the job even better. Experiment with cranks and

crawlers to find out. In the cool waters of fall, try running cranks and crawlers at the same relatively slow speeds—say 1.2 to 1.4 mph. For the lures themselves, it's hard to beat Rapala Husky Jerks (in shallow and deep-running versions), Tail Dancers, and Shad Raps. Again, match the colors to the prevalent baitfish and conditions—silvers around shiners and shad, brighter fluorescents in darker or stained water. You can use reflective tape to trick out your lures with additional color. Add a strip of silver or glow to the lure's sides, something that's particularly effective at night.

If the structure is particularly steep or difficult to follow, you might want to try lead core. I like it if I'm on a break that twists and turns and I'd have too much line out with boards. Even in 45 feet of water, you can often get down to the fish zone with 75 to 85 feet of lead line out.

For rods you're going to need something substantive enough to handle heavier snap weights or lead core—an 8-foot, 6-inch model has a limber enough tip that tends not to tear out hooks. Still, you can get away with weights up to 4 ounces (say, if you're bottom bouncing next summer) or heavy-pulling cranks.

More than anything, targeting fall walleyes is a matter of perspective. While it's easy and familiar to stay close to structure, that's not always where the fish are. Open your mind to the possibility of roamers and suspenders, and then go looking for them. They could be half a mile away from your favorite reef or hump. But you'll never know unless you try it.

Opposite: Once you find a structure where walleyes are hanging out, pull out your map and look for more of the same areas. DAVID ROSE

CHAPTER SEVENTEEN

On the Drop

Fall walleyes concentrate on the breaks with twists and turns. You should be there, too.

When the weather cools with the onset of fall, the summer stability that once allowed walleyes to go anywhere and do anything they wanted—go shallow, go deep, or suspend—is a thing of the past. (At least until next year.) Starting now, the vast majority of walleyes in any given system will be close to the first drop-off, either on the shallow side or off a ways in deeper water. For one thing, the fish are concentrated; for another, all the options of summertime are unnecessary in the simpler times of fall.

When walleyes return to the main drop and its vicinity, there's essentially a reversal of spring patterns. The fish position themselves on spots of hard bottom, around clumps of weeds, and near creeks. With the simpler locational preferences the fish show, I go with a simpler method of presentation. For the most part I can bet on jigging to do the trick. The reason is that jigging targets the precise spots where the walleyes are holding better than anything else. Now is the time when the biggest

In the fall it's a good bet to fish corners and cups along a weed breakline. DAVID ROSE

decision you have to make is whether to pitch or to vertical-jig—excellent methods both. The decision depends on what depths you're targeting and what you see on electronics.

Corners and Cups

The best sort of spot I know is a turn in the breakline—a corner or a cup, it's often called. The easiest way I know to find breaklines when clear water conditions allow is with polarized glasses. When I put the glasses on, I'm often able to see the breakline plain as day, and more than anything I look for points with turns that form the corners and cups. They are the key spots for fall walleyes, whether the fish are shallow, on the flat, or out deeper around 20 feet of water. Also, when there's a point on land, I check either side for deeper water.

The other way to find such turns, when your vision is not enough, is to follow the drop-off with quality electronics. Get in the shallows and head out until you see the bottom start to taper off. Say that happens at 12 feet. Then it's time to turn and follow the drop at 12 feet, watching on electronics for where it veers out to a point or in closer to shore. When you're slowly motoring down a break next to a wide flat, the optimum spot is where the break swings in toward the flat, affording deep water and a pathway where the walleyes can go from deep to shallow. With modern electronics it's possible to spot pockets of hard bottom and tufts of weeds—additional features that concentrate walleyes and are well worth your attention.

Another way to locate breaklines and turns is to check out a quality contour map—a tool that shortens the search on any water. First I look for flats represented by widely spaced contour lines. That's a feeding flat that will probably have weeds and other cover. Next I look for tighter contour lines, ones that are closer together, that indicate a sharper drop. I don't focus solely on flats, though. I also check any main-lake structure, be it a point or a sunken island, for similar contour lines that indicate deeper water with a sharp break.

Horizontal and Vertical

When the search is done, it's time to start catching fish. Most of the time I start on the shallow side, on the flat and the first drop. One of the fastest ways to search with a jig is with a plastic bait—say, a 4-inch jigworm, grub, or minnow. With no-stretch six- or eight-pound flame Berkley FireLine, I'm able to rip a ¼-ounce jighead through weeds and see the line for any ticks of a walleye taking the bait. To work the plastic, I cast out, let it sink to bottom, and snap the jig in 1-foot lifts. Most of the strikes occur when the bait falls.

Often, after I've located where the walleyes are holding with plastic, I'll go around and fish more methodically with live bait. I'll pitch to the same stretch of flat and drop-off with a jig, most times a ⅛-ouncer, and a minnow. After you've caught the more aggressive fish on plastic, which is an excellent search tool, it makes sense to comb the water more thoroughly with bait.

Many times, though, the walleyes are beyond the drop-off, hanging in deeper water. While it's often difficult to spot fish on electronics in 10 feet or less (but perfectly possible to spot weeds and hard bottom), walleyes are easier to see in deeper water. If the fish I mark are in 15 feet of water or more, I'll sit on the front deck of my boat and run my bowmount electric to slip with the wind through the fish and jig vertically. Once fall starts, I'm going to stick with a minnow most of the time in deep water. One reason is that with FireLine you can feel the minnow jump around when a walleye stares it down. When that happens, I give the motor more juice so that I can hover over the fish and keep a jig in its face. Often I'll have to sit in one place for a couple of minutes until the walleye takes the bait.

Electronics are indispensable to help you figure out whether those walleyes are in 15 feet or 25. Whichever it is, I'm still looking for the turns in the break where fall walleyes concentrate. So pitch shallow and drop straight down in deeper water. The jig is up with the onset of fall.

CHAPTER EIGHTEEN

Evening to Night

Every evening, walleyes make movements like clockwork.

Every evening, when light gives way to night, walleyes make movements like clockwork, shifting their position from deep to shallow, with a spell spent in between. They start out over and around structure, slip onto the edges, then slide atop the flats. When the fish are in motion with nothing more than short stopovers, you had better be, too.

Knowing how to pattern the fish and their nocturnal progressions, along with the timing of their movements, will keep you on walleyes when other anglers are sitting on spots that shut down hours ago. But you must change more than your location. You need to follow the fish from different levels in the water column with offerings that are better suited to low light and are most appropriate for the shallows and their edges. Add the right gear and boat rigging to the mix, and you'll be prepared to stay with the walleyes long after dark.

Night Moves

Starting in evening, a very popular fishing time, walleyes will still be in daytime mode. They'll be on or adjacent to main-lake structure such as underwater islands and reefs close to deep water. Sometimes the fish will be right on the bottom at 10, 12, or 15 feet; other times they'll suspend nearby at the same depths in over 50 to 80 feet of water.

The most effective way to locate them is by pulling a spinner and nightcrawler behind a bottom bouncer. If the water's clear and lacks obstructions, you can get away with a 6- or 7-foot leader. If it's darker and snaggy, shorten up to maybe 2 feet. You can also add rattle beads for added attraction. For the suspended fish, switch to trolling planer boards with clip-on weights of ½ or ¾ ounce run 30 to 80 feet behind the boards, depending on how deep the fish are. Experiment with line length until you hit the right depth.

As soon as twilight arrives, be ready to abandon the earlier areas. Now I begin to search shoreline-adjoining structure near deep water. Try points, reefs, drop-offs, and weed beds. The fish won't show up all at once, but

A stealthy approach for shallow walleyes is a must. DAVID ROSE

they'll begin showing up gradually. More of them will arrive as it gets darker. At this time, I focus on 8 to 15 feet of water—staging areas before the walleyes move shallow. It seems as though the walleyes are getting their bearings. You can often see the fish on a locator, but you don't want to run over them with the gas outboard and then try to go back to fish them in the shallow water. They'll be gone. But you can scout them out and return later.

Here I go after them primarily with crankbaits. Crawler harnesses still work and can often be excellent, but too often I have to fight off other kinds of fish, including sheepsheads and bullheads. Harnesses can keep up with cranks but seldom outproduce them. That's why I prefer the cranks on spinning tackle with six- or eight-pound FireLine. My favorites are Rapala Husky Jerks in both the shallow and deep-diving versions. I add a piece of reflective tape to them for added visibility. I also paint a thin strip with glow paint around the head and tail to help the walleyes zero in on the bait.

To work them, I cast out, crank the lures down, stop, pull the bait forward, stop, and repeat. That's about all there is to it. At times you'll want to vary the length of the pauses, letting the bait rest for ten, fifteen, even thirty seconds. Experiment till you find what the fish want. Know that a strike will often be nothing but a "tick." If you feel it, be sure to set the hook.

Beyond twilight, walleyes will move shallower yet, into 3 to 6 feet of water. The most productive all-around depth range, though, is 5 to 10 feet. The same areas apply—just move shallower. I like to cast Husky Jerks but will often switch to trolling to cover water. To move the bait slowly, I put my bowmount trolling motor on low speed—just fast enough to make the bait wobble. But here I switch to a No. 13 Original Rapala with a split-shot for weight ahead of it.

Again, a strike won't be more than a "tick." For that reason, I like to troll the Rapalas on twenty-pound Berkley FireLine for its lack of stretch and extreme sensitivity. A solid baitcasting rod allows you to pick up line and better set hooks.

Now that you have the right stuff and the knowledge of the walleyes' whereabouts, you'll be ready to find fish with confidence and comfort. When you're out there looking for fish during the evening-to-night transition, don't let the fish come to you. Keep searching so that you can keep up with the fish's movements.

CHAPTER NINETEEN

Now and Later

Find green weeds to catch fish in fall and the future.

Starting with the onset of fall, it always pays to look for green weeds. Lively weeds that haven't faded in color—and have therefore retained their capabilities to produce oxygen and harbor baitfish—hold walleye all the way until the ice forms. The patches you find now might be top producers even into next year.

In the upper Midwest, two kinds of weeds stand out. Cabbage weed is a tall plant with broad leaves. It's crispy, too, and fairly easy to fish because you can rip a lure through it. Coontail, on the other hand, looks like a raccoon's tail, with bushy stems that are tougher and gnarlier. They still hold walleyes but are more difficult to fish. Either way, I'm going to look for deep water nearby—say, water over 20 feet and patches of weeds near the drop-off. Even if I find green weeds on a shallow flat, I'm probably going to skip them if they're a quarter-mile or more away from deep water. Indeed, all weeds are not created equal—and, we'll soon find, neither are the ways in which you fish them.

Find 'Em First

Weeds in and of themselves are good things. Weeds in close association with other underwater elements are even better. For instance, in addition to deep water within a reasonable distance, I'm going to look for weeds close to points and humps—important features that concentrate walleye. When fall is approaching or well under way, green weeds on the tip of a point or on the edge of a hump are going to concentrate walleyes for some of the best fishing of the year.

While weeds often grow close to the surface and can be spotted with the naked eye, a couple of other strategies help detect them. Wearing a quality pair of polarized sunglasses cuts glare and helps me see the dark spots that indicate weeds. To check the greenery, I'll pitch a cast in there and see what I pull up. If the weeds are brown and slimy, I skip them; if the

I check for walleyes on my electronics as I slowly cruise the weed edge. DAVID ROSE

weeds are green and fresh, I'm going to probe them for a while. Another method to search out weeds that aren't visible from the surface is to motor around and look with your depth finder. Weeds might come a few feet off bottom but not even make it close to the surface—potentially an excellent spot.

Atop the Greenery

How you go after walleyes depends on whether you're going to target them atop the greenery or on the edge. The walleyes that get atop the weeds seem to respond to wind or to the low light of morning or evening. The first way I'm going to look for them is to cast a minnowbait, such as an Original Rapala or a Husky Jerk, and I'm going to match its color to whatever kind of food is in the lake. For example, I'll use black and silver around shiners and gold or natural perch color around perch. I also give the baits frequent pauses when I retrieve them—twitching them, stopping, and repeating. To get a little closer to the weeds but just above them, I'll cast a ¼-ounce jighead with a soft-plastic grub or swimbait, such as a Northland Mimic Minnow, and retrieve it at a speed where it occasionally ticks the tops of the weeds. If it catches weeds, I snap it free—more easily done with no-stretch Berkley FireLine than stretchy monofilament—and speed up the retrieve.

Another great way to target walleyes atop the weeds is with a slip-bobber and minnow. I set the stop so the minnow, rigged on a jighead or a colored hook, rides a foot or two above the weed tops. Most times I put a couple of split-shots—say, No. 7s—a couple of feet above the jig to keep it from rising toward surface if the wind skates the bobber away. (Leeches are another good choice in September; the water gets too cold to inspire action come October.)

On the Edge

On the edge of weeds I'm apt to use of mix of live bait and artificials. To present a bait on the fringe, I'm going to run my trolling motor to keep me on the edge or slightly beyond it. I'll fish a jig with a minnow vertically

under the boat, or I'll fish a live minnow, such as a sizable chub or shiner, on a slip-sinker rig.

Then again, I often fish jigging spoons or plastic tails on jigheads. I boost up to a size slightly larger than I might use for a jighead with a minnow; so if I'm jigging with a minnow and a ¼-ounce jig, I'll go with a ⅜-ounce spoon. Cast it toward the edge of the weeds, let it sink to bottom, and when it hits, rip it upward. Let fall back to bottom, and when it touches down, rip it again. You can do the same thing with jigheads with plastic tails. Cast out a jighead—match the weight to the depth—and a grub or minnow tail; then, when it hits bottom, snap it up and let fall back to bottom. Work it all the way back to the boat; when the jig gets beneath you, jig it vertically a few times before giving up on it and reeling it in for another cast. Often walleyes will follow a jig back toward the boat but not commit until the last moment.

Green weeds are good stuff. They hold walleyes well into fall. And if you remember their location or, better yet, mark them on GPS, you can try them again once the lake ices over later in the year. Find 'em now to catch 'em now—and later.

Opposite: Vertically fishing creek chubs just on the outside of a weed edge usually yields good results. DAVID ROSE

WINTER

CHAPTER TWENTY

Hard-bottom Highways

The last place you find walleyes in fall is the first place to get them through the ice.

Remember where you last caught walleyes in the fall? Good. That's because the last place you found them in open water will be the first place to get them through the ice.

Consider the classic fall pattern—deeper fish in daytime, shallower ones at dusk and into dark. The same progression holds true once a lake seals up, and the more exploration you did in a boat, the better the chances that you'll have the knowledge of not only the underwater terrain but also the walleyes' movement around it. With memory, shoreline sightings, and GPS coordinates, the chances of finding and catching walleyes are far better—even if the ability to move is limited compared with open-water angling. But despite the tendency to stay put when it's seemingly a lot of work to punch new holes and try new spots, a measure of mobility is essential to keep up with the walleyes on what I call the hard-bottom highways.

Steep and Deep

In winter, and in walleye fishing in general, change is good. The most productive flats, points, drop-offs, and deepwater basins have varying degrees of depth and cover. On flats, a few patches of green weeds could do the trick. On a drop-off there might be little points or a scattering of gravel. The depths leading to the shallows, meanwhile, might have little ribbons of hard bottom. I call such areas hard-bottom highways because these strips and patches of hard bottom are the thoroughfares that walleyes travel from the depths at midday to the edges of points and humps at the late-evening witching hour.

Because of this predictable pattern, I do my homework when I can still get my boat out, watching with electronics for hard bottom leading to the edges where everyone is staked out come twilight. You can catch fish all day if you know the travel routes the walleyes use. For instance, I'll motor around an area and look for the brighter colors that indicate

The split screen helps zoom in and enlarge the bottom—see the same picture on the graph on both sides of the screen. But note that on the left the two fish on the hard bottom leap out at you, where you have to look hard to see them on the right-hand side. DAVID ROSE

hard bottom. Then I'll punch them into my GPS unit and later punch the coordinates into a handheld Lowrance unit to find them again when ice fishing. The hard bottom could be hundreds of yards away from where you'll be working the edge of a point at prime time, but the little patches will be just what it takes to hold fish hours before prime time.

Steep drop-offs from shore are another type of area I always consider. The reason is that they afford the fish easy access to shallow-water feeding grounds. One fall I caught a bunch of big walleyes in Michigan's Upper Peninsula, on small lakes with steep shoreline drop-offs. There I cast big creek chubs on live-bait rigs to the edge of a visible drop-off, then worked the rig down into the depths, finding fish scattered at varying levels. I knew the same areas would hold fish come first ice.

While it's tempting to take all your equipment out on the ice and hunker down for hours, I try to get an earlier start and follow the walleyes into their prime feeding zones on the edges of points and flats. And it's always best when I have knowledge of the adjacent areas, or GPS coordinates, to help me locate them through the ice. I'll start deep and start drilling. One of the best assets for my approach of covering hard water is a power auger.

Raps and Reality TV

Much of my ice angling is done with the venerable jigging Rapala, but I've learned a lot from ice experts around the United States and Canada to make slight modifications to produce more fish. One such trick, which is similar to what I've done for years with my favorite night-trolling bait, the No. 13 Original Rapala, depends on knot placement. While I've long cinched the knot on the underneath of the eyelet with the stickbait to provide greater roll and wobble at slow speeds, I've learned from some ice savants the importance of playing with knot placement on a Jigging Rap. A snap is great, of course, for changing out lures. It is possible, however, to catch more fish with the knot cinched at the back of the Rap's eye to provide a different look and swimming action underwater. Try it.

I've also learned a lot from watching walleyes and other species on an underwater camera. Over decades of ice fishing, I've developed the jigging tricks that perform the best. With a camera, it's now possible to watch your very own reality TV—and to find what fish like and what they don't. Walleyes, for instance, are attracted to a Jigging Rap, but sometimes getting them to commit can be another story. I've learned to jiggle the Rap and slowly lift it above their heads, which is often just what it takes to get them to "open sesame."

I've done a lot of experimenting with fluorocarbon lines, jigging spoons, and other offerings. In clear water I've definitely caught more fish on fluoro, which is essentially invisible underwater and has far less stretch than monofilament for quality hookups. If the water is somewhat murky from currents that are common on the Great Lakes and even inland waters, I'll try a spoon with brass rattles that call in fish from a distance. I like to tip the treble with a minnow head.

I suppose it would be tempting to put up a shanty and wait out the walleyes. But with the knowledge gleaned from their fall patterns and the mobility that comes with a quality auger and portable shanty, there's no reason to hunker down for a short-lived burst of action at nightfall. It's time to start traveling the walleyes' own hard-bottom highway.

CHAPTER TWENTY-ONE

First Ice

When the lakes freeze in walleye country, you don't have to look far for the top spots to target.

Yes, the last spots that produced walleyes in fall are the best bets for a couple of weeks after first ice. But you can no longer cast, no longer troll, no longer cover water in the traditional sense.

Now is the time it pays to have prime late-fall locations saved with GPS coordinates or, at the very least, with detailed shoreline sightings. Then it's time to burn holes in the ice with a quality auger—the closest thing to covering water. With holes staggered deep, shallow, and atop prime spots, you'll have the versatility to cover the all-important migration routes walleyes travel. Offer the fish both a jigging lure and a jig with live bait, and you'll have the right stuff to tempt them, no matter their mood.

Underwater Trails

The locational similarities between fall and first ice occur whether you're 4 miles out on Saginaw Bay, 8 miles out on Little Bay de Noc, or 100 feet out on an inland lake. The principles of finding the same contour and same key spots, then setting up precisely atop them and all around them, hold true wherever you are.

Thanks to GPS, I have the ability to return to the exact spot I fished before the lakes sealed up with ice. But when a group of us goes fishing, I drill holes all around that key location. With a power auger I'll get my holes drilled—at least dozens and perhaps fifty of them—right away to keep from making noise later.

Without GPS and all the holes, finding the key spots would be difficult. But with both the GPS and the auger on my side, I can first find a drop-off, point, or rock pile, then cover every inch of it. Some of the most important areas are well off the structure, over deep water. That's where walleyes often hold for most of the day before sliding in shallower at twilight to feed in earnest. Instead of waiting atop a rock pinnacle almost all day until a late flurry, it's possible to catch them during daylight by prospecting up to a hundred yards away. When I drill a hole, I normally give it thirty to forty-five minutes to produce before moving to the next one. Most important is knowing the underwater trails where walleyes ease from deep to shallow; this way, you'll be able to follow them on up when they move.

Another key piece of equipment is an underwater camera. After all, you want to be fishing for walleyes, not suckers. With a camera I can see the fish I'm marking on a liquid-crystal unit and identify them. And I get a better idea of their migration routes. One winter on Little Bay de Noc, in Michigan's Upper Peninsula, our holes were on a line of old net stakes from commercial fishermen. On the camera I could see the walleyes and perch move from one stake to another in their travels. The camera also allows me to see which motions I impart to my lures pique the walleyes' curiosity and which ones spook them off.

Twitches and Tackle

Wherever I am, the first lure I turn to is a No. 5 or a No. 7 Jigging Rapala with a minnow baited on the treble. The Rap is an excellent lure for drawing fish in—something you'll find out when you catch them or spot them on the camera. To complement the Rap, try an ice spoon tipped with a minnow. Use it on another rod set atop a bucket next to you and let it sit. The live minnow will provide enough subtle action to get fish that come in for the Jigging Rapala and peel off to eat the minnow on the other rod.

It's too easy to get caught up in aggressive jigging motions similar to what you'd use in open water. With the Rapala I go slow and easy, jiggling the lure about a quarter inch to half an inch. That's it. Every now and then I'll lift the lure up a little higher to try to draw walleyes in. Then I return it to the position it was at a moment earlier and keep on jigging.

Pay attention to the camera to find out what fish like. I have, and with the camera I've noted that walleyes like the jiggle.

In winter with a short rod, it helps to have stretch-free line to set hooks. Remember, if your rod is a couple of feet long, a short lift doesn't take much to send the hooks home. That's why I use no-stretch six-pound Berkley FireLine, especially in water deeper than 30 feet. Otherwise I'll use fluorocarbon, which has less stretch than monofilament and is practically invisible in clear water.

Between jigging a Rap and setting up a dead rod, you'll have the bases covered for first-ice walleyes. Just be sure to be in a key late-fall spot with a lot of holes drilled. If you're mobile enough to find the walleyes and follow them up their underwater trails, you'll be in the right place at the right time—in other words, the perfect combination when location, presentation, and season unite.

Opposite: After pinpointing my summer hot spot with my GPS, I am ready to turn it into my winter hot spot. DAVID ROSE

95

CHAPTER TWENTY-TWO

Stay or Go?

Move around, or pick a spot and wait—some of each pays dividends for winter walleyes.

When ice-fishing for walleyes, there are places where it's best to set up camp and stay put. There are others that lend themselves to a base camp from which to make forays in every direction—deeper, shallower, and in the same depth.

With both approaches, it pays to be quiet and efficient—to get your holes cut, make the most out of the lines you're running, and choose quality baits and lures that come in the form of both the time-honored and the latest and greatest. All together, efficient ice fishing is one part strategy and another part efficiency. Let's do it...

Take Me to the Rivers

For starters, the time of year gives an indication of walleyes' whereabouts. First ice in December or January, depending on where you live and fish, finds the walleyes closest to the places they last occupied in open water. Some examples: steep breaks, deep edges of main-lake structure, and drop-offs adjacent to feeding flats. Now the walleyes are going to be moving closer to the places where they're going to spawn—for example, near river mouths, on and around the edges of hard-bottom flats, and any structure in the form of humps and points near either of the above.

What next? I like to make a decision, often through scouting and searching, about where to set up shop and how mobile I ought to be. A hump in reasonable depth, near a river mouth— say, within a half mile or so—often warrants a daylong stay, for walleyes will often filter through from morning till evening. The same goes for the most important corners of humps or points. I like the places that drop off sharply into deep water or have a cluster of rocks to hold fish or bring them in. On the other hand, I like to spread out, or at least have that possibility, in areas that are flatter and more tapering—in other words, slower tapers with fewer breaks and turns to concentrate walleyes.

Ross Grothe shows what happens when you pull it all together. DAVE SCROPPO

One of the best indications of what's happening down below is an underwater camera. With it you'll be able to see the bottom and see if it has any rock, any bait or, for that matter, anything to concentrate walleyes. Or you might see a few cruise through. Walleyes on the move often mean it will make more sense to spread some lines out—send someone in your party on the same breakline, someone else deeper.

A portable fish house then lets you react to what you're seeing or react based on the time of day. For instance, I'll pull a portable out to deeper water (sometimes 40 feet or more) during the middle of the day. There I like to jig for walleyes that are either on the move or lazing before moving to their prime haunts on the edge of the break and other structures come morning and evening.

Most times I'll set up on the key piece of structure—say, on a weed patch or hard bottom on the break—and then drill holes in every direction. The beauty of a quality auger is that you can get your holes cut efficiently, let your noise diminish, and get to business.

Good Looks, Hot Rods

Perhaps no lure is more dependable or time-honored than the Jigging Rapala. Even so, Rapala has introduced a Jigging Shad, a ⅛-ounce jigging lure with a wider body more similarly shaped to a shad. With either of them I typically tip the bottom treble with a minnow head, or I hook a minnow through the head on the treble and run a stinger hook down to the minnow's tail. Meantime, you can't go wrong with the tried-and-true Northland Buck-Shot Rattle Spoon. Here, the same thing goes: Tip the treble with a minnow head or minnow, and drop it down.

That's even more the case when you're able to move around with a quality portable shack and a lightning-fast power auger. Set up camp on key spots with steep breaks. Go exploring on flats where walleyes tend to spread out. A little versatility goes a long way for ice fishing.

CHAPTER TWENTY-THREE

Size Matters

Larger visual cues are usually better when attempting to attract and trigger.

Size matters in walleye fishing, and winter is no exception. But while the tendency is to try smaller baits and lures, larger visual cues are usually better when attempting to attract and trigger fish. And though they sometimes won't trigger, large lures consistently draw fish into the neighborhood, where they can be caught with methods other than jigging. A tip-up? Check. A bobber rig? You bet. A deadstick? Go get 'em. Which is to say, the time is right for two-timing walleye.

Consider when and where decent-size baits—larger than average lures—excel. Troll in spring on Lake Erie, and you're going to be pulling No. 12 and No. 14 Rapala Down Deep Husky Jerks. (The No. 12 measures 4¾ inches.) Fish at night, and I've found that the most consistent bait for walleyes small and large is the No. 13 Original Floating Minnow because of its profile (5¼ inches). The same principle of bigger is better extends to ice-fishing season. Set a monster sucker on a tip-up for pike, and don't be surprised by the monster walleye that eats it. While I love diminutive

For a great payoff, drill lots of holes right away so you can move up or down the structure as the walleye move. DAVID ROSE

No. 5 Jigging Raps through the ice, I've seen No. 11s ring the dinner bell, with the whole lure inhaled by walleyes, particularly on the Great Lakes.

What's more, a little bit of versatility to drill plentiful holes will provide a lot of latitude in the depths covered. Fish locators and underwater cameras, meanwhile, will indicate how walleyes are responding to the size of the bait as well as its action. Go big, or stay home!

Drill, Baby, Drill

For starters, you're going to need holes in the ice. When drilling, I like to start on the edge of structure and, from there, head for deep water, where walleyes lie during midday before ascending to the edges with morning and evening.

When holes are drilled and a fish house put up, it's time to get busy. I do it with a combination of GPS and fish-finding capabilities, both of which unite in a single, portable unit that not only gets you there (and back) in the event of a whiteout but also spots your lure and any fish visiting to inspect it. Switch to full-screen LCD flasher and ice mode, which displays large targets (say, walleye or pike) in reds and yellows, baitfish or jigs in blues and blacks. Lift your jig up to the fish's level, jiggle, and enjoy.

With the sonar as well as an underwater camera, you'll get to see how walleyes respond to your jigging motions. Twitch it hard and you can bet they'll bail. Jiggle it gently and they're probably going to eat. If they keep looking without biting, reel up slowly, above their heads, and keep jiggling. If the fish back off, drop down again to where you're seeing them and start over again.

The Deadstick: It's Alive!

Fish finders and underwater cameras are going to show you fish. That's great info to have. The reason: If the walleyes aren't responding to jigging methods, you can employ others. A tip-up with a shiner hooked behind the dorsal with a light-wire treble is a good one. (Suspend the bait a foot or two above bottom.) Otherwise, take a Northland Fire-Eye Minnow—a long, thin jig similar to a spoon—and bait a minnow through the lips. For this extra deadstick, I'll lean the rod against a bucket or go with a slip-bobber to show me bites. (You'll catch some big walleyes with this rig.) The jigging with a Rapala attracts them, and if they won't eat it, you can bet they're going to grab a piece of bait subtly presented on a deadstick.

When you're ice fishing, start out big and see what happens. A big Jigging Rapala will often draw in the walleyes—and get them to whack it. When they won't eat it, though, bust out the deadstick. It's a regular whuppin' stick when you get the walleyes revved up with a bigger bait.

CHAPTER TWENTY-FOUR

Frozen Fish Tricks

Carry an assortment of jigs and spoons— some are better for aggressive fish, others for less-aggressive ones.

At any given time, on any given day, it's hard to say how ice walleyes will respond to the lures and colors you're putting in front of them. That's why I always carry an assortment of jigs and spoons in assorted shades. With them, my group of friends who are fishing together can try every variable to see what's working best. Through the process of elimination, we can switch over to the hot bait and most effective retrieve. Some are old standbys, some open-water weapons. But whichever ones we're talking about, it takes the right moves to make them work their magic.

The Jigging Rapala

Come wintertime, no other bait is as widely used and trusted throughout walleye country as the Jigging Rapala, a lure that has almost no action on its own. That part's up to you. Too many people, however, overwork the Jigging Rapala and catch too few fish. But compared with the other jigs and spoons we'll be talking about, the Rapala is still the most aggressive lure, one that requires fewer and shorter pauses than any other ice offerings. In the Midwest the most effective Raps I've found are the No. 5s and No. 3s, which look like perch lures. Don't worry, though. They'll catch everything that swims, including big walleyes.

But you have to manipulate them with the right motion to do the trick. When working a Jigging Rapala, the most important lesson is not to twitch it. No, this isn't like working a jig in open water. Instead the proper action is a lift and a drop—a smooth, not herky-jerky, motion. Simply lift on a tight line, then lower on a tight line. Seldom do I move the lure more than 6 inches, and often I barely lift it an inch.

That's it for the action, but there are a few tips that will make the Rap work even better. For starters I like to fish the lures on an abrasion-resistant monofilament line. A foot above the lure I tie in a ball-bearing swivel to prevent line twist and attach the lure with a snap for a better swimming motion. For added scent and flavor, I'm a fan of a piece of minnow on the middle hook, which is a treble, or a minnow tail on the back hook. If you're fishing inland waters, don't overdo it with a big chunk of bait; but if you're on Lake Erie, you can put a whole minnow on every hook. Looks crazy, I know, but trust me and try it.

Spoons

If nothing's happening on the Jigging Rapala, it's safe to say that the fish are less aggressive—Raps work best when the walleyes are in a happy mood. To match my offering to more neutral fish, I always go with a small, 2- to 2½-inch spoon. Of all the spoons out there, I've found none that outproduce Northland's Fire-Eye Minnow. The compact lures come in great colors and are easy to fish, working better at slower speeds with more frequent pauses. Here the most important lesson is to pause for as long as you've just twitched the lure. It's the movement that attracts walleyes and the pause that seals the deal. Just don't overdo the action. Twitch the spoon—yes, bait it with a piece of minnow—a few inches at a time, then hold it steady.

One nuance of the approach is touching bottom with the spoon. Do you want to? Some days, yes; some days, no. I try to give the fish the option by watching what everyone else is doing and then trying the opposite. At times the walleyes will want nothing to do with a lure that's banging bottom. Other times they'll jump all over it. You'll only find out if you try.

Dead Rods

As a complement to other jigging approaches, the best way to liven up the action is often a dead rod. A dead rod? You bet. That means one that's just sitting there, no extra action involved. I believe that active lures like Rapalas and semiactive ones like spoons will draw fish in, but they'll turn their attention to something slower. That's why I always have an ice rod with a Northland Fire-Ball jig hanging in one hole. I simply bait it with a live minnow and let the jig sit a few inches above bottom. Okay, sometimes I'll walk over and give it a little wiggle, but that's about it. Simply put, most folks don't use plain leadhead jigs through the ice often enough. And I've seen them produce time and again, especially on Saginaw Bay when walleyes were tough to come by with any other technique.

Finally...

A couple more tips will help you catch more fish through the ice. With them, you'll complement your jigging approach with some hard-won wisdom I've learned over the years. First, don't be afraid to fish deep. By deep I mean 30 to 45 feet. The fish are often there earlier in the day prior to the faster bite at twilight in shallow water. But watch with electronics for suspended fish, which will be up higher seeking better oxygen content. To further "lure" walleyes to your ice holes, try baiting with a little bit of dog food. You can simply drop some in a hole or, better yet, put some in an onion sack with a couple of rocks. Tie it up, drop it down on a piece of line, and let the dog chow draw in the baitfish. The walleyes won't be far behind.

Opposite: When you're 3 miles off-shore and it's –11 degrees with a 15 mph wind, you better be prepared to keep comfortable.
DAVID ROSE

CHAPTER TWENTY-FIVE

Going Deep

Worry not if fishing water as deep as 30 and 40 feet defies conventional thinking.

Wherever and whenever I go ice fishing, I never underestimate the importance of going deep. It's always easier, of course, to hike less instead of more to reach a potential fishing hole. Besides that, most anglers I know are more comfortable in shallower water. Water as deep as 30 and 40 feet—beyond the humps, points, and flats so attractive to conventional thinking—can seem a no-man's-land.

But that's just the territory I seek out for walleyes whenever it's available. In late winter, deep water is the home of big fish. Not just any deep water will do, however. I like to set up adjacent to prime twilight feeding areas in the 20-foot range, where the predators filter in from the depths. The abyss is where it's at.

Food First

Trout fishermen are fond of saying that big ones don't get that way by sipping insects their whole lives. True, magnum stream trout are carnivores that eat minnows and small trout. The same thinking goes for pike—the big ones are not the residents of the weeds that dine on finger food, if you will. The largest pike in any lake cruise the depths, mowing down walleyes, perch, ciscoes, and whitefish—in other words, mouthfuls. Likewise, decent-size walleyes don't eat insects their whole lives when substantive baitfish are available.

The food connection is why your best bet in midwinter is in water between 25 and 40 feet deep. And that's why I go wild when drilling holes—I want to cover as much of that deep water as possible.

Though the water is deep, it still makes sense to get your noise over with when you get out on the ice by drilling your holes all at once. And when you drill more instead of less, you'll have options for covering water. I like to start at the tip of a point and put a hole every 10 yards out from it until I reach 40 feet of water. Or I follow the edges of any structure—say, a hump or deep flat. Like deer, fish travel in predictable routes. This way you'll intercept fish on their movements from deep to shallow.

To give me an idea of what presentation makes most sense, I pay attention to an underwater camera, which lets me see what species are beneath me and then lets me adjust my responses accordingly. When walleyes visit, I can slow down and start jiggling my bait.

Even in winter, walleyes are aggressive and in search of big baits. I catch a lot of big walleyes on No. 11 Jigging Rapalas, a sizable offering. Or try a spoon with rattles. Either way, add a minnow to sweeten it, or go without bait. Watch on a camera to see how walleyes respond. I'll also jig more aggressively than ever for walleyes, even ripping the bait a foot at a time to draw them in. When it's cloudy, try bright baits like firetiger. Under brighter conditions, go with more natural blacks, blues and silvers.

At the other end of the spectrum are tip-ups with live minnows. For a shot at a monster walleye, I'll find the biggest minnow in the bucket and set it 18 inches off bottom below a tip-up. Sure enough, walleyes are consumers, not connoisseurs.

If you go deep, you'll have your best opportunity of the year to winch one in when it smashes a jigging lure or trips the tip-up flag.

Walleyes: One Twitch Too Many

While some walleyes dart in and strike like there's no tomorrow, others sneak in and suddenly appear on an underwater camera. One twitch of a lure too many and they're gone.

That's particularly true of walleyes outside the twilight witching hour, when the fish are most prone to forgive jigging sins. Deepwater fish at midday, on the other hand, can be downright cranky. With the fish finder and underwater camera, I've monkeyed with the same fish for up to fifteen minutes before it will bite. When I'm twitching a Jigging Rapala with a minnow on the treble, I'll bring the fish I see on the camera and locator upward, reeling a crank of the reel and continuing to jiggle the bait. When a fish follows, keep it coming upward. When it quits on you, drop back to bottom and begin again. For maximum action, attach your jigging lures with a plain snap, not a snap swivel. For minimal twist, put a ball-bearing swivel 18 inches above the lure.

One of the best ways to get the midday fish is to keep drilling holes beyond your shanty—as far away as you can stand to get. That's been the most effective approach in places like Little Bay de Noc, in Michigan's Upper Peninsula. If my shanty is in 34 feet of water, 300 yards away the depth might be 38 or 39 feet—just enough extra depth to hold fish that are less pressured than the ones in close.

As the ice season progresses, you don't have to give up the depths, but be sure to get closer to potential spawning grounds. (Heck, I've caught males that were milting in almost 40 feet of water in mid-February.) Walleyes commonly spawn under the ice, and their seasonal movements are good evidence of their spawning interest. To follow their progressions, I'll find a deep mudflat close to rock, gravel, and rivers. Often the walleyes will hang in the mud during the day and move in to the rock or the river mouth toward evening. When you have all your holes drilled ahead of time, it's easy enough to fish deep during the day and move in shallower when evening comes. The walleyes might even turn on in the depths—a reason to have a group of anglers trying different levels to determine the prevailing pattern.

With a little attitude adjustment, it's possible to get over any aversion to deep water. Come to think of it, your first big haul of walleyes is going to do it for you.

Opposite: Setting up on jagged snow-covered ice is better than on clear ice you can see through, because it doesn't allow as much light through. Walleyes like lower light conditions. DAVID ROSE

CHAPTER TWENTY-SIX

Great Lakes versus Inland Ice

Supersize it on the Great Lakes; away from the inland seas, subtle is the way to go.

It's often said that walleyes are walleyes wherever they swim. That's true for the most part, but one of the few times there's a noticeable difference between populations is when you're ice fishing—specifically, when you compare walleyes from inland waters with their big-water brethren of the Great Lakes. Although similar principles apply wherever you fish, the techniques with which you catch ice walleyes had better be supersized on Lake Erie, Saginaw Bay, and the Bays de Noc. Away from the inland seas, subtle is the way to go.

In a way, inland versus Great Lakes walleyes represent a tale of two fishes. Through the ice on lakes and reservoirs, it's hard to beat little lures with a piece of bait or a small minnow. On the big water, though, you can gob up a spoon or a Jigging Rapala with a minnow—a pretty big one, at that—on every hook. Big-time predators, open-water fish accustomed to mowing down shad and alewives, simply like it large. Come winter, paying attention to the walleyes' tendencies and giving them what they want are going to mean more fish.

Drilling Your Holes

Wherever you fish, it's important to drill your holes and make your noise as quickly as possible. To get a spread of holes that allows me to fish shallow, deep, and in between, I drill as many holes as possible over productive water. For starters I look for large, flat areas near some current—prime feeding territory. It's important that the flat is near deep water so that the walleyes don't have to roam far to feed. When punching holes, I put them out in the depths over soft bottom, on the edge of the drop, and atop the flat. Even better is hard bottom such as gravel atop the feeding flat.

Whether I'm on inland waters or the Great Lakes, I rely on electronics to find key areas. On inland waters I might take my GPS coordinates from open-water fishing to pinpoint a rock pile or a gravel patch on a point. I'll also pay attention to hard bottom or sharp turns, write down the GPS coordinates, and then go out with a handheld unit to find the spot below the ice. Combine the edge of hard and soft bottom with a little bit of current, and you're in business.

Another option is green weeds. The brown ones that are dying give off carbon dioxide—not the right choice. Green weeds give off oxygen and hold insects and baitfish, which in turn attract walleyes. Just be sure not to drop an offering too far down into the weeds. Elevate it just enough to stay above the weeds, where the walleyes move in to feed.

Small or Supersize?

Now comes the time to trigger the fish. On inland waters I always downsize my offerings. Instead of a No. 5 Jigging Rapala, I opt for a smaller No. 3. The reason is that you're dealing with smaller baitfish and less-aggressive walleyes than the Great Lakes predators that chase down big mouthfuls over vast stretches throughout the year. Likewise, I'll downsize with lighter line—say, six-pound test—and incorporate a subtle second rod. While I jig a Rap or a spoon, I'll have a dead rod with a jighead or a simple plain hook with a split-shot with a minnow. That second rod will often catch the fish that come in for a look at the jigging lure but opt for a minnow that's just sitting there.

Other lure choices when I'm inland are Northland's Fire-Eye, a cross between a jig and a spoon, and the Forage Minnow, another crossover that sits horizontally in the water. The Forage Minnows come in holographic colors, which is important in clear water. In clear water I like colors such as holographics or black and silver or blues. If the water has more stain, I'll switch to firetiger and bright orange. It never hurts, either, to add a little bit of scent—perhaps some Dr. Juice—for inland or Great Lakes walleyes.

When chasing Great Lakes monsters, I'll beef up accordingly. I'll use ten-pound fluorocarbon instead of six pound or switch to ten-pound Berkley FireLine, which has little stretch to set hooks into big fish and the abrasion resistance to wrestle them through the hole, which would shred most monofilament. For lures I immediately go with a No. 7, No. 9, or No. 11 Jigging Rapala. For better hookups I switch the treble to one size larger, and at times I'll add a FireLine stinger to nab short strikers. For Great Lakes fish I put a big minnow on that treble, or sometimes I'll put a minnow on each of the treble's hooks as well as the ones at the head and tail of the Rap. Another way to bulk up the profile of a jigging lure is to cut the minnow in half and thread the head on the front hook and the tail on the back hook. Try it. When using rattle spoons—noisy offerings that draw walleyes from a distance—I put a minnow on each hook.

Wherever you fish, it's important not to overdo the jigging motion—a lesson I learned from watching walleyes on my underwater camera. While short strokes of a few inches draw walleyes in, very seldom does the same jigging motion trigger them. When you spot walleyes that come in to investigate, on either a camera or a liquid-crystal fish finder, immediately slow down your jigging. That's when I seldom give the lure more than a shake or a jiggle. Most of the time I can get the walleye to bite by slowing down. If the walleye doesn't commit, I slowly reel the lure up and keep jiggling and reeling—I've had walleyes nail a lure 6 feet below the ice over 30 feet of water.

This is where fish finder enters the picture. Since an interested walleye will chase a lure out of camera range, you need a fish finder to see if a fish keeps following. If it does, keep raising the lure and jiggling it. If the fish won't commit and plummets back to bottom, drop your lure back down and start the process over again. When the walleye again shows interest, keep bringing it off the bottom. Sometimes you have to play cat-and-mouse with a walleye for as long as fifteen minutes. This approach works both inland and on the Great Lakes, though it excels with open-water predators in places like Lake Erie and Bay de Noc.

For a complement to my jigging lures, I'll put down a plain leadhead jig, normally a ⅛- or ¼-ouncer, with a minnow. Many times, particularly on Saginaw Bay, a plain, unpainted jighead with a minnow hooked through the lips is just what the walleyes want.

Just what the walleyes want… On inland waters it's usually something small and mellow. On the Great Lakes it's normally something big and garish. And when you match the lures and accompanying baits to the walleyes' prevailing behavior, you're going to have the right stuff, whether it's subtle or supersize.

CHAPTER TWENTY-SEVEN

Ice and Open Water

In the fickle Midwest, it's possible, even probable, to have ice and open water at the same time.

On the cusp of spring, a frozen surface remains on lakes while floes dissipate from rivers. And it just so happens that the time is right to get in on serious prespawn walleye movements in either domain.

There's a surprising similarity between the two despite the seemingly at-odds environments. In lakes and rivers, walleyes are on the move, migrating before the spawn. Their locations are far different from months, even weeks, earlier. Knowing where walleyes will be and how to target them makes all the difference between poor fishing and some of the best of the year.

Frozen Ice Heating Up

This is the time of year of late ice, when walleyes are approaching their spawning grounds. Come late February and into March, I seek out areas near creeks as well as spawning flats such as gravel and rock reefs—places where walleyes will spawn before long. The fish move through in waves, shallower than they've been for the previous months. While 30 to 50 feet of water was the deal earlier, now I'm looking as shallow as 8 feet, with my preferred depth range of about 15 to 30 feet.

Keys at these depths are changes in bottom composition. It helps to have transitions from soft to hard bottom, especially mud to rocks, gravel, and hard clay. The reason is that these spots have more underwater life—more "stuff" growing on them that, in turn, attracts bait.

Mark Brumbah proudly displays the fruits of his use of an underwater camera. DAVID SCROPPO

It's easy to see this correlation with an underwater camera. When you drill holes and put a camera down, you'll find areas where minnows scoot across bottom from rock to rock. The walleyes are never far behind. I see both bait and predators with my underwater camera, which allows me to figure out why one hole might be more productive than others. There's always a reason, including food or cover in the form of rocks or bottom debris. The cameras are also handy because you can find out how the fish react to a given jigging motion. To offer a shortcut, I've found that aggressive jigging more often than not spooks walleyes. They like it slower and gentler, with frequent pauses. Something more aggressive will draw them in but seldom get them to bite.

Spoons and jigs are the best bets for locating fish and continuing to catch them. Northland's Buck-Shot Rattle Spoons call in walleyes from a distance with rattles that are particularly effective in water with a bit of stain. If it's clear, be sure to try holographic colors that trigger walleyes without spooking them. I usually bait the spoon's treble with a piece of minnow for scent and flavor. If I'm on the Great Lakes, where the fish are huge and unabashed, I might hang a minnow off each hook of the treble. Don't overlook jigs, though. A plain leadhead or a rattle jig actively worked in your hand or set as a deadstick is a tremendous option. If I'm jigging a spoon with one rod, I always have a deadstick out with a minnow just inches above bottom. Often I'll bring fish in with the spoon, but they'll take the jig.

Go with the Flow

Jigging is not lost on river rats who hit the open water as soon as it's safely possible to dodge icebergs. I'm right there with them.

Similar to the patterns on lakes, river walleyes will be moving in from connecting waters such as the Great Lakes in anticipation of spawning. Baitfish will be on the move as well—another cue for migrating walleyes. In clearer rivers walleyes will be deeper, at the heads, sides, and backs of holes. They'll be along drop-offs and channel breaks. In darker rivers walleyes will scoot into the shallows—water as thin as 3 feet—where they're concealed by the turbulence.

Whichever I'm fishing, I always look for warmer water. Discharges from power plants and other kinds of industry may raise the water temperature a couple of degrees, which is enough to concentrate a hot pod of walleyes. Creeks accomplish the same thing as they flow through farmlands and boost the temperature when they enter the river. The warmer water alone is enough to concentrate fish. If you have cover, it's even better. Fish the upstream side and behind rock piles or bumps and depressions on bottom. Be sure to watch on quality electronics for such nuances, and get your bait down in any hidey-holes where walleyes are hanging.

Indeed, electronics and tackle are important ingredients when river fishing. On quality electronics with high definition, it's possible to see the slightest bumps on bottom—and fish behind all around them. I'm always certain to anticipate a rise in bottom by watching the electronics, lifting a jig above it, then dropping it down the back side, where walleyes hold out of the current.

One of my favorite offerings when vertical jigging for spring fish is the same rattle jig I use when ice fishing. As I've seen so many times, especially when the water's turbid or the fishing pressure's heavy, the rattles are that little something different that triggers strikes. To bulk up an offering for bigger fish and to present a softer mouthful, I'll hook on a 3-inch Berkley Power Minnow. The chartreuse ones are dynamite on all river systems I've fished. Most of the time I'll add a minnow, too, but plain plastic works great on rivers—sometimes better than bait. Have one angler in the boat use plastic, another use bait, and let the fish tell you what they want.

When it comes time for fishing on the fringe of spring, it can be a little difficult to figure out what *you* want to do. Ice or open water? Me, I'll take some of each. The walleyes, you see, are moving in anticipation of spring, and I'll go wherever necessary and do whatever it takes to catch them.

Simplicity Is a Virtue

With the many different ways to catch walleyes, it's heartening when you consider the ways to clean and cook your catch are best when they're straightforward and unadulterated. That's why my overarching belief on both subjects is simplicity. When you think about it, the driving force motivating a walleye is food. It's first among the fish's urges, with spawning and other desires farther down the list. Beyond the intrigue of how to catch them, not to mention the thrill of competition, the inexorable compulsion to pursue them is deep within the fiber of my being. Not unlike the walleye, food tops my list, and the finned curiosity overwhelmingly influences my every move—not only the catching, but the eating.

The route from water to dinner table naturally begins on the water. Once the catching's accomplished—that's the fun part—it's time to care for your catch. The easiest, most no-nonsense method is in the aerated live well of my Lund boat, where the captives receive a regular tonic of fresh water and air bubbles to keep them lively. But even before I enjoyed the onboard luxury of multiple live wells many moons ago, I too fished from a rowboat, where storing fish was a far cry from where we are today. Even so, my grandfather and father never encouraged use of a stringer. Any such tether allowed the fish to thrash, bruise, and die in short order—all of which let a walleye start to spoil. Instead, the Martin patriarchs taught their son that the best way to keep fish in optimum condition for the table was on ice.

As a result, they always brought a cooler full of cubes to keep our inevitable catch. They taught their son right. When we'd fish into the wee hours and I'd wind up falling asleep on cushions and life preservers—that's what a whippersnapper would do—they'd wait till noon or early afternoon the next day to clean them. With fish stored on ice, chilling them to prevent against spoilage or deterioration, the first step when one gets home is a thorough rinse to remove accumulated slime.

Then, whether they're jamming in captivity of the live well or somnolent from a long sleep in the big chill, the next step is cleaning. (That said, I dispatch live ones by conking them on the head with the butt end of a steel

Enjoy the simple goodness of walleye, grilled according to the recipe from Chief Papineau—see page 123.

with which I touch up my knives; place the fish belly down on the cleaning station; and give them a sharp whack between the eyes.)

Of all the ingredients in the cleaning, the most important is a quality knife. A friend of mine has had the same Rapala fillet knife since boyhood, and that was more than thirty years ago. That's what you get when you care for a knife made of superior steel. Among the attributes of the Rapala or any other quality knife are the ability to hold an edge, flexibility to do the precision work of removing rib bones, and sturdiness in the butt section of the blade. The Rapala knives deliver on all accounts.

For walleyes under 20 inches, the 6-inch blade is most comfortable to me. For larger fish, I like a larger knife—the 9-inch offering is my choice.

The proper knife makes it easier to fillet walleye. NORMARK RAPALA

Even so, I like to release a lot of the fish over 20 ticks. The meat is coarser and not so sweet as with the little ones. Yet my friend Chief Papineau taught my friends and me an excellent recipe for grilling fillets atop a piece of brown bag soaked well in olive oil. Check out his novel—and delicious—technique in the subsequent cooking section. His method is ideal for Great Lakes magnums, which are often strongly flavored due to a diet of alewives and other strong-tasting forage.

My preference is simply to fillet the fish and remove the rib bones. If you've caught a bunch and have extras, now's the time to prepare, freeze, and store them. The best way I've found is to wrap the fish in plastic for a protective coating and then place in a plastic bag for an extended stay in the deep freeze. They taste best when cooked within two months. To thaw them, leave in the refrigerator overnight.

Now comes an additional thought process—and more opportunity for creative thinking. That'd be selecting simple, tasty recipes that let the walleye's flavor emerge. Each fillet of a 15- to 20-incher weighs in the neighborhood of 4 to 6 ounces. What follows are some of my favorites.

PAN-FRIED FILLETS

Go easy, young angler. There's no need for unnecessary monkeying with walleye cooked in a shallow bath of hot oil.

⅓ cup oil, or enough to fill pan ¼ inch deep (I prefer peanut oil for its ability to withstand high heat)

6 walleye fillets, skinned, each cut into thirds

1 cup fish batter (your commercial favorite or all-purpose flour seasoned with a mix of paprika, freshly ground black pepper, and kosher salt)

1. Heat oil on high until it just begins to smoke. It will first shimmer before it starts to smoke. Be ready for the signs.
2. Dip fillets, with their natural moisture, into the dry batter until thoroughly coated.
3. Place fillets skin-side down (though the skin has been removed, place flesh side that once had the skin face-down in the oil) for approximately 2½ minutes, until golden brown. Turn and repeat on opposite side.

It's imperative not to overcook the fish and allow it to get dried out. A light, golden brown should indicate the proper mixture of doneness and moisture.

Serves 4.

SACRIFICE-FREE TARTAR SAUCE

Too often, tartar sauce is gloppy, overly gluey, and sickly sweet. Enter my favorite, which I've tricked out with extra lemon juice and fat-free plain yogurt that, despite fewer calories, tastes far better than anything I've ever had in a restaurant.

1 cup mayonnaise
½ cup plain, fat-free yogurt, drained of liquid for at least 30 minutes through a strainer lined with paper towel
1 medium barrel pickle (sour, not sweet)
⅛–¼ cup capers, depending on taste, minced
Juice from 1 lemon
2 green onions, both green and white parts sliced thin

Mix all ingredients and allow flavors to marry for at least 15 minutes.
Yield: 1½ cups. Will keep, refrigerated, for 3 to 4 days.

BEST BAKED WALLEYE

In keeping with my overarching philosophy of simplicity in fish preparation, I keep my baked walleye downright straightforward and unadulterated, with few extra flavors and not much in the way of sauces.

Cooking spray or olive oil
4 small to medium walleye fillets, approximately
Salt, pepper, and paprika to taste
Basil pesto (optional)

1. Preheat oven to 350°F.
2. Spray foil-lined baking sheet with cooking spray or smear with a tablespoon or two of olive oil.
3. Place fillets skin-side down and sprinkle with herbs and spices. Brush with pesto, if you like.
4. Bake for approximately 10 minutes.
Serves 4.

CHIEF'S GREAT GRILLED WALLEYE

Since walleye contains scant fat—less than 1 gram for a 3-ounce serving, compared to almost 4 grams for an equal amount of beef, according to U.S. Department of Agriculture data—it's seldom considered a great grilling fish, unlike salmon or various saltwater species containing a considerable amount of oil. Unfortunately, grilled walleye is prone to drying out, its sweet, mild, toothsome texture commonly approximating balsa wood. But my friend Kim "Chief" Papineau, a fellow professional angler, once fed a group of us grilled Great Lakes fillets, which so often taste fishy due to their overwhelming diet of baitfish. Not so with Chief's innovative technique of outdoor cooking. They turn out moist, tasty, and mild.

Walleye fillets, rib bones removed, with skin and scales left on
Paper grocery bag
Olive oil
Cajun seasoning, to taste

1. Cut the paper sack into sections just larger than fillets, then soak with olive oil (either on a deep-lipped plate or in a zipper-type plastic bag), allowing paper to absorb oil thoroughly.
2. Preheat grill and place the fillet skin-side down onto oil-soaked paper; drizzle or spritz meat with a light coating of olive oil, then sprinkle with Cajun seasoning.
3. Place fillets atop paper onto preheated grill (the oiled paper sizzles but doesn't burn), cover, and cook for 10 to 15 minutes, or until meat flakes with a fork.

Bon appetit!
Serves 4.

HOBO PACK WALLEYE

Another excellent way to keep grilled walleye from drying out without drowning it in butter is in a foil pouch. This technique of cooking meat is widely credited to campfire cooking done by scouts groups—hence the name "hobo packs." It's also outstanding with fish, and despite its inherent simplicity of form and function, cooking fish in a foil pouch is incredibly refined, given its similarity to the French technique called *en papillote*. Translation: in paper.

Fish wrapped in foil accomplishes the same as using parchment paper, with fewer leaks, less mess, and comparable flavor and succulence. Talk about simplicity. Just wrap fish fillets in a foil envelope and bake or grill over medium to medium-high heat.

4 to 8 walleye fillets
2 lemons, sliced ¼ inch thick
Salt and freshly ground pepper
½ cup dry white wine or vermouth
¼ cup extra-virgin olive oil
Carrots, red peppers, and/or green onions, sliced thinly lengthwise

1. Preheat oven to 400° F or grill to a similar temperature. Cut foil into 12- by 12-inch squares equal in number to fillets on hand.
2. Divide lemon slices onto the foil squares. Place fillets on the lemons and sprinkle both sides of the fish with salt and pepper.
3. Fold sides of foil squares upward to make boxes around the fish.
4. Pour a splash of wine or vermouth, along with 1 tablespoon of olive oil, into each foil box.
5. Divide vegetables among packets.
6. Fold the sides of packets around the fish, as if wrapping a present.
7. Bake or grill 10 minutes and serve.

Be careful when unfolding the packets to avoid being scorched by the steam. This technique works well with all manner of fish fillets and steaks.
Serves 4.

SEVICHE: THE RAW AND THE COOKED

For an alternative to the ordinary, try a Walleye Country variation on a Peruvian appetizer called seviche, in which raw, firm-fleshed fish is marinated in lime or lemon juice and seasonings. But here's the catch: The fish isn't cooked—at least not with heat. It's "cooked" by marinating in citrus for 24 hours. Walleye fillets are perfect for this technique. To adjust the dish to your tastes or to boost flavor, experiment with additional ingredients such as crushed red pepper, green chilies, scallions, or the zest of a lime. In the interest of food safety, know that it's wise—and suggested by many food safety agencies—to freeze the fish for 48 hours before marinating to kill any parasites.

2 pounds walleye fillets, cubed, frozen then thawed
4 lemons, juiced
2 limes, juiced
5 or 6 dashes Tabasco or other hot-pepper sauce
½ red onion, minced
1 jalapeno, minced (remove seeds for less heat)
¼ cup cilantro, minced
Black pepper, to taste

Marinate fish cubes for 24 hours in mixture of all ingredients.
Serves 4.

STEAMED AND STIR-FRIED

Flaky, white fish such as walleye is ideal for steaming and brief stir-frying, resulting in a low-fat dish with clean, light flavors. Thin whole fillets can be steamed in the same way as the cubes in the following recipe. The spice selection is open to your interpretation. Red pepper flakes would be perfectly suitable for a spicy heat after you remove the lid.

1 tablespoon canola oil
¼ cup dry sherry
3 green onions, sliced thin
3 tablespoons soy sauce
1 clove garlic, minced
3 tablespoons grated ginger
4 fillets, cubed
Cooked rice

1. In a small bowl stir together oil, sherry, green onions, soy sauce, garlic, and ginger. Spread evenly atop fish cubes.
2. Heat dry wok until hot and add fish and vegetable mixture. Stir a few times to coat bottom of wok with fish and liquid, then cover with a lid and steam for 15 minutes.
3. Remove lid and allow fish to brown and green onions to crisp around the edges, approximately 3 minutes. Serve over rice.

Serves 4.

A Beautiful Mind

Even David Letterman had to get his start somewhere. Decades ago, the wiseacre of a local weatherman in Indiana congratulated a tropical storm on its promotion to a hurricane. Another time he reported hail the size of canned hams. The pop-culture icon is proof positive of life before the big show.

Me? I was a welder in a furniture factory. Now I make my living, focusing tireless efforts, around walleye fishing. In fact, I've done just that for more than two decades.

In many ways, walleyes were still in their formative years when I made the break to full-time fishing in the late '80s; but with two decades of momentum since, the sport—competitive and otherwise—is reaching a fever pitch. Enormous tournament fields, lured by first-place purses well into the six figures, are filled with hundreds of hopefuls. Pioneering vast, walleye-filled waters, boats and motors have grown to proportions that shrink big, tempestuous seas, including the Great Lakes, down to size and have helped to extend summertime interest to the rougher periods of spring and fall. Further boosting the fascination are burgeoning Great

Lakes fisheries following the Clean Water Act and efforts by many states to spike the punch with stocking.

Like them or not, tournaments have had a significant impact in the development not only of more seaworthy boats but also of tackle and tactics, including the proliferation of artificial offerings such as crankbaits and soft plastics. No matter the time, place, or inclement weather, my colleagues and I have to catch them.

Then there's the challenge that comes with the walleye's adaptability to a range of waters from Dakota reservoirs, to the Midwest's natural lakes, and through the immense Great Lakes, to say nothing of the species' special mystique. Let's face it: The fish just looks cool, like a mysterious ghost with white eyes. In freshwater, walleyes are perhaps the most diverse fish you'll find. They'll be in 6 inches of water or suspended over 100 feet. What they present to us anglers is a monstrous challenge, like a 10,000-piece puzzle.

Now is the time to crack the code. Wherever, whenever you go, walleyes are swimming into a diversity of patterns. Fish hard; fish smart; fish with the latest, greatest techniques in Walleyedom. (Ever smoke the walleyes on plastic worms?) Just be careful. You don't want to lose the day job if you can help it. Or maybe you do…

Even so, catching walleye isn't a slam dunk—truth to tell, far from it. If anything, walleye lack the pyrotechnics of other species. There's no eruption on a surface lure, behavior displayed by bass, for example, or various saltwater aggressors with stiletto teeth, vibrant colors, and bursts of speed to 30 mph. None of that from my drab brown and ochre antagonist, a subsurface feeder that doesn't fight worth a lick and is prone to bipolar mood swings that have them opening sesame one moment and alternately clamping it shut. Walleyes, I say, are the most challenging fish because they can be so ignorant and stupid at times. You go out the next day, and they're gone or they aren't biting.

If the munch and crunch of bass and saltwater fishing are analogous to the monster mash of professional athletics such as basketball and football, I liken walleye angling to baseball, a game of strategy and subtlety that is certainly not for everyone. Too boring, some say. Too many long, elaborate silences for an end result lacking dramatics. On the other hand, I groove on the idiosyncrasies and the process, the ultimate in problem solving to figure out when—and if—the fish want to eat, say, an artificial lure or a live

bait. If they want to eat within 10 feet of the surface or belly to the bottom. If they're turned on by twinkling junk jewelry—say, purple and pink beads from Jo-Ann Fabrics—ahead of a night crawler or greater realism in the form of lifelike minnow imitations bestowed by their manufacturers with naturalistic silver shades, lifelike perch patterns, and holographic renderings for the ultimate in verisimilitude. Then again, there are times when live, spirited minnows presented on a gossamer thread of invisible fluorocarbon leader material are the ticket.

Indeed, walleye can be unequal opportunists for either the real thing or the best-laid plans of artificial intelligence. What with the walleye's mind games, it's anyone's guess which will work under the circumstances—one reason I can't get enough of my favorite finned adversary.

On the bright side, you can eat walleye in good conscience. They are at once stocked in copious numbers and spawned with additional, sufficient propensity to top off the state-created menu like a goblet of tiramisu. To keep and eat a wild stream trout, on the other hand, would pretty much put you on the sex offender registry. Given the prevailing ethos of catch-and-release, trout are practically protected by constitutional amendment. Don't ask, don't tell isn't going to cut it. Someone's going to find out, somehow, and you'll end up an outcast for it. Carry a wicker creel off the river and risk bodily injury; fill a live well with a limit of walleye, and you'll be a hero at day's end at the boat launch when bystanders ask what's biting. Heroism in the kitchen is a guarantee, too, whether it's with fresh walleye fillets fried in batter and hot peanut oil, sautéed in ground pistachios and clarified butter, even "cooked" with citrus in the Latin American fashion of seviche.

Well, where would our national pastimes be today without the forward pass, the jump shot, or the split-finger fastball? *History!* We've come a long way, after all, since Bob Cousy's jumper started to supplant basketball's time-honored set shot. That was then, this is now, and I'm ready to face new sporting challenges if you are.

So, let's keep motivating—and innovating—well into the new millennium.

Opposite: Hog walleyes like this one make me smile—and often make me a winner—at weigh-in time at tournaments. DAVID ROSE

INDEX

ABOUT THE AUTHOR

Growing up in northwest Michigan, Mark Martin learned to fish for walleye, perch, salmon, and trout from his father and grandfather. Mark currently lives in Twin Lake, Michigan. His granddaughter, Delaney, is learning to fish from the master. Mark is now teaching her how much fun it is to participate in the outdoor world by bringing her to the best fisheries at the best time, so she's getting bites and having fish on. Now she can fight giant fish and get them in the net.

Mark has been a professional walleye angler since 1985, when he began fishing the Masters Walleye Circuit (MWC). In 1990, with the start of the *In-Fisherman* Professional Walleye Trail (PWT), Martin won the first PWT Championship on Lake of the Woods, Baudette, Minnesota. He is in the all-time top-ten in dollars among PWT money winners and qualified for seventeen of eighteen championships.

Author of the books *Year-Round Walleyes* and *250 Walleye Tips*, Mark also produced the video *Night Walleye Fishing*. In addition, he has appeared on such TV programs as *In-Fisherman, Michigan Out-of-Doors, Wisconsin Waters and Woods, Denny Geurink's Outdoor Adventures, Angler's Diary, Practical Sportsman, Ron Schara Outdoors*, and *Midwest Outdoors*.

Eight-year-old Delaney shows off one of many salmon she has caught by herself. MARK MARTIN

Besides tournament fishing, teaching seminars, and leading kids fishing clinics, Mark is an outdoor educator whose knowledge frequently appears in *In-Fisherman's Walleye In-Sider, Outdoor Life, Fishing Facts, Midwest Outdoors, Michigan Woods-N-Waters News*, and other periodicals. He also teaches walleye wisdom around North America as he travels to compete in tournaments.

Get more secrets from the pros in these fine Pro Tactics™ books:

Pro Tactics™: Bass

Pro Tactics™: Catfish

Pro Tactics™: How to Fish Bass Tournaments

Pro Tactics™: How to Fish Walleye Tournaments

Pro Tactics™: Ice Fishing

Pro Tactics™: Muskie

Pro Tactics™: Northern Pike

Pro Tactics™: Panfish

Pro Tactics™: Steelhead & Salmon

Pro Tactics™: Tackle Repair & Maintenance

Pro Tactics™: The Fishing Boat